# Classroom Observation Tasks

# CAMBRIDGE TEACHER TRAINING AND DEVELOPMENT

**Series Editors: Marion Williams and Tony Wright**

This series is designed for all those involved in language teacher training and development: teachers in training, trainers, directors of studies, advisers, teachers of in-service courses and seminars. Its aim is to provide a comprehensive, organised and authoritative resource for language teacher training and development.

**Teach English** – A training course for teachers
*by Adrian Doff*

**Models and Metaphors in Language Teacher Training** – Loop input and other strategies
*by Tessa Woodward*

**Training Foreign Language Teachers** – A reflective approach
*by Michael J. Wallace*

**Literature and Language Teaching** – A guide for teachers and trainers
*by Gillian Lazar*

**Classroom Observation Tasks** – A resource book for language teachers and trainers
*by Ruth Wajnryb*

**Tasks for Language Teachers** – A resource book for training and development
*by Martin Parrott*

**English for the Teacher** – A language development course
*by Mary Spratt*

**Teaching Children English** – A training course for teachers of English to children
*by David Vale with Anne Feunteun*

**A Course in Language Teaching** – Practice and theory
*by Penny Ur*

**Looking at Language Classrooms**
A teacher development video package

**About Language** – Tasks for teachers of English
*by Scott Thornbury*

**Action Research for Language Teachers**
*by Michael J. Wallace*

**Mentor Courses** – A resource book for trainer-trainers
*by Angi Malderez and Caroline Bodóczky*

# Classroom Observation Tasks

A resource book for language
teachers and trainers

*Ruth Wajnryb*

CAMBRIDGE
UNIVERSITY PRESS

PUBLISHED BY THE PRESS SYNDICATE OF THE UNIVERSITY OF CAMBRIDGE
The Pitt Building, Trumpington Street, Cambridge, United Kingdom

CAMBRIDGE UNIVERSITY PRESS
The Edinburgh Building, Cambridge CB2 2RU, UK
40 West 20th Street, New York, NY 10011–4211, USA
477 Williamstown Road, Port Melbourne, VIC 3207, Australia
Ruiz de Alarcón 13, 28014 Madrid, Spain
Dock House, The Waterfront, Cape Town 8001, South Africa

http://www.cambridge.org

First published 1992
Eleventh printing 2002

Printed in the United Kingdom at the University Press, Cambridge

Typeset in Sabon 10/12pt

Library of Congress catalogue card number: 91-33131

A *catalogue record for this book is available from the British Library*

ISBN 0 521 40362 6  hardback
ISBN 0 521 40722 2  paperback

# Contents

# Thanks

The relationship between teaching and learning is a complex and fascinating one, generating ironies as well as beauty and reward. The overwhelming impression in my mind today, after more than twenty years' work as a professional teacher and teacher trainer, is how much I have learned from those I set out to teach.

In their own ways, the diverse groups of people with whose education I have variously been involved, have contributed to the knowledge base of *Classroom Observation Tasks*. I therefore gratefully and respectfully acknowledge my current and former language learners, trainee teachers and trainee trainers, as well as teaching colleagues, for their role in my learning and in this book.

# Acknowledgements

The author and publishers would like to thank the following for permission to reproduce copyright material:
J.F. Fanselow and Cambridge University Press for the extract from ' "Let's see": contrasting conversations about teaching' by J.F. Fanselow on p. 12; Longman Group UK Ltd for the extract from 'Observation for training, development or assessment' by P. Maingay on p. 14 and the questions adapted from *Lessons from the Learner* by S. Deller on p. 120; the National Centre for English Language Teaching and Research, Sydney for the extracts from 'Learning to teach: four instructional patterns in language teacher education' by D. Freeman on p. 15; Oxford University Press for the extract from *Aspects of Language Teaching* by H. Widdowson on p. 45; the United States Information Agency for the extract from 'A system for improving teachers' questions' by J.W. Tollefson on p. 48; V. Zamel and TESOL Inc. for the extract from 'Cybernetics: a model for feedback in the ESL classroom' by V. Zamel, 1981, TESOL Quarterly, 15, 2, Copyright 1981 by TESOL, reprinted by permission on p. 51; S. Lindstromberg and *The Teacher Trainer* for the extract from 'Teacher echoing' by S. Lindstromberg on p. 52; Heinemann Publishers (Oxford) Ltd for the extract from 'Are trainees human?' by R. Gower and S. Walters on p. 101; T. Woodward and *The Teacher Trainer* for the diagrams adapted from 'Observation tasks for pre-service trainees' by T. Woodward on p. 107; Newbury House/Heinle & Heinle Publishers for the adapted extract from *Teaching Languages: A Way and Ways* by E.W. Stevick on p. 108; R. Brown and *The Teacher Trainer* for the adapted extract from 'Classroom pedagogics – a syllabus for the interactive stage?' by R. Brown on p. 112; D. Nunan and Cambridge University Press for the extract and material from *Designing Tasks for the Communicative Classroom* by D. Nunan on pp. 130–132.

# Part One  Introduction

## 1  Observation as a learning tool

### Observation for learning

This book is about observation as a learning tool. It is about being an observer in the language learning classroom and learning from the observation of classroom processes.

Being in the classroom as an observer opens up a range of experiences and processes which can become part of the raw material of a teacher's professional growth. This book is designed to show teachers how to use these experiences to learn more about their own teaching. It aims therefore to make observation in the classroom a learning experience. This is done by providing a bank of tasks which guides teachers through the process of observing, reflecting and drawing conclusions.

Observation is a multi-faceted tool for learning. The experience of observing comprises more than the time actually spent in the classroom. It also includes preparation for the period in the classroom and follow-up from the time spent there. The preparation can include the selection of a focus and purpose and a method of data collection, as well as collaboration with others involved. The follow-up includes analysis, discussion and interpretation of the data and experiences acquired in the classroom, and reflection on the whole experience.

It is important to say at this point that observation is a skill that can be learned and can improve with practice. It is often assumed, somewhat naively, that the ability to learn through observing classroom events is fairly intuitive. In fact, while few would deny the role of intuition in the preparation of teachers, the ability to see with acuity, to select, identify and prioritise among a myriad of co-occurring experiences is something that can be guided, practised, learned and improved. It is a major aim of this book to encourage these types of learning processes among beginning and practising teachers.

Let us see the wealth of learning that observation affords by considering: (1) who observes; and (2) for what purpose.

### Who observes?

Observation can serve a number of people in a number of contexts

1

towards a number of different ends (see Fig. 1.1). This book is addressed mainly to *classroom teachers* engaged in observation as part of their professional development. The observation may be initiated either by the teachers themselves or by the school, as part of a school-based support programme for teaching staff, or beginning teachers, or newly-employed teachers engaged in an induction period. Other observers include:

- *trainee teachers* who observe teachers, other trainees and trainers as an important part of their own initial training process;
- *teacher trainers* who observe trainees teaching;
- *teacher developers* who observe teachers as part of a school-based support system;
- *trainee trainers* who observe teachers and trainee teachers.

### For what purpose?

There are a number of different purposes for observation. However, the primary one considered here is teachers' professional growth and development. Our aim is to give some guidance or structure to the process of observation.

Observation for assessment, such as that which takes place in pre-service teacher training courses or during probation periods or for employment-related matters, is not dealt with here. As it is usually value-based, directive, externally imposed, and coloured by factors not necessarily related to learning, it does not fall within our central notion of observation as a learning tool. Also, as this was the traditional, and often sole, reason for observing teachers and classrooms in action, it is an area that has previously received a lot of attention. Observation as a learning tool, on the other hand, is quite a recent development in the literature of teacher preparation and education.

## 2 Who is this book for?

This book is designed to interest and serve a number of people involved in language teaching. They are:

- the teacher;
- the trainee teacher;
- the trainer;
- people involved in school-based support (e.g. co-ordinators, senior teachers, heads of school);
- people involved in trainer training, whether in universities, teachers' colleges or private institutions.

| Context | | Observer | Observee | Purpose of observation | | | Samples of observation experiences |
|---|---|---|---|---|---|---|---|
| | | | | Training process | Ongoing development | School-based support | |
| The contexts of in-service and school-based teacher development | 1 | Teacher | Peer teacher | | ✓ | | Two teachers observe each other's teaching as part of a mutual self-development venture or project |
| | 2 | Teacher | Peer teacher or Senior teacher | | ✓ | ✓ | A teacher observes another teacher (peer or more experienced) in response to a perceived need to develop in a particular area |
| | 3 | Teacher coordinator/ developer | Teacher | | ✓ | ✓ | A teacher invites a teacher developer to observe his/her teaching as part of school-based teacher support |
| The context of pre-service training | 4 | Trainee teacher | Teacher | ✓ | | | A trainee observes an experienced teacher as part of the classroom experience module of the course |
| | 5 | Trainee teacher | Teacher trainer | ✓ | | | A trainee observes a trainer teaching as a 'modelling' experience |
| | 6 | Trainee teacher | Peer trainee teacher | ✓ | | | Two trainees observe each other within the practical teaching component of the course |
| | 7 | Teacher trainer | Trainee teacher | ✓ | | | A trainer observes a trainee for diagnostic and support purposes |
| The context of trainer training/ development | 8 | Trainee trainer | Teacher | ✓ | ✓ | | A trainer-in-training observes teaching as part of systematic training in identifying and prioritising teaching behaviours |
| | 9 | Trainee trainer | Trainee teacher | ✓ | ✓ | | A trainer-in-training observes a trainee teacher as part of the practical component of a trainer training course |

*Figure 1.1 Contexts and purposes of classroom observation*

The observation contexts which this book seeks to support are:

- pre-service teacher training;
- school-based teacher support;
- teacher development;
- trainer training/development.

These contexts may or may not co-occur within the one teaching institution.

In Section 5 (see pages 17–26), more specific guidance in how to use this book is offered to the various groups of people listed above. For the moment, let us examine the broad aims of these various groups and how *Classroom Observation Tasks* is addressed to them.

### The teacher

This book is addressed primarily to the teacher. The person we have in mind is someone who has completed an initial, pre-service training programme and is now working in a language teaching context. This might be English language teaching ('second' or 'foreign') or modern language teaching; with children or adults; in private schools or government institutions. It may be taking place in a target language speaking context (such as teaching English in an English-speaking country) or in a context where the target language is not spoken outside the classroom (such as teaching English in Japan, or French in England). In fact, neither the context of teaching nor the amount of teaching experience that the teacher has had is a constraint to users of the book. What *is* important is that teachers involved are interested in teaching (particularly their own) and in the various processes that occur and co-occur in language classrooms, and are motivated to engage in some structured tasks that will allow them to explore teaching in the areas of their interest and choice.

The teacher may wish to engage in some informal or semi-informal observations. These may be initiated and implemented by teachers in a collaborative effort. Alternatively, they might be structured in some way by the support offered by the school (see *School-based support*, page 23). Another situation may involve a teacher engaged in a course of in-service study, a component of which involves a programme of peer observation.

*Classroom Observation Tasks* seeks to provide stimulus and ideas for ways of exploring one's own teaching by observing other teachers and classrooms in action, or by having one's own teaching/classroom observed for the purpose of continued learning and exploration.

For further information on how observing the classroom is linked to teacher development, see page 8 and pages 18–19.

## The trainee teacher

Some trainees begin a pre-service teacher training course with some experience of the classroom, perhaps as a teacher of another language or perhaps as a primary-school teacher. Others have never before stepped into a classroom in the shoes of a teacher. Whatever the teaching background of the trainee, all have had educational experience in classrooms and hence they come to training with some expectations. These might be conscious or subconscious, or a blend of the two; they might be positive or negative; they might imbue the trainee with courage and optimism or with nervous apprehension or dread. Whatever the cargo of experiences and expectations that a trainee brings to a training course, one thing is certain – that the classroom has primacy of place in the learning and teaching experiences that lie ahead. It is important that these experiences are used in the process of learning to become a teacher.

Classrooms, however, are complex arenas where many processes co-occur and overlap. It takes a skilled and trained eye to perceive, understand and benefit from observing the proceedings of learning/teaching. This book is intended both to provide training in the skills of observing and to help trainees to understand and learn from their observations by making the experience of observing personally meaningful. The tasks in this book can be used for observing fellow trainees, experienced teachers or teacher trainers.

## The trainer

The task of the trainer is to help the trainees understand the various processes involved in the teaching and learning of a language and the complex array of activities that occur in a language classroom. The classroom therefore should play a key role in the training process. This book is intended to serve as a bank of classroom experiences which will complement other components of the training course.

The tasks can be used by teacher trainers as a part of their training sessions in a variety of ways. For example, all trainees could be given the same task to carry out, and the results compared in a plenary session. Alternatively, individuals or groups could do a task and prepare a presentation summarising the results for the rest of the class. This can in turn lead to a discussion of the theoretical issues arising from the area of focus.

## School-based support personnel

Many teachers are fortunate to be working in contexts that have various mechanisms of school-based support. This may take different forms – for example, a co-ordinator system in which a co-ordinator supports and guides teachers in the selection and implementation of a curriculum; a teacher development group; a senior staff member responsible for a programme of professional development; a head teacher keen to upgrade and support the skills of the teaching staff. This book will assist those people involved in providing school-based support by supplying mechanisms for allowing observation of classes to become a means of learning.

Regrettably, professional development sometimes amounts to one-off lectures given by a visiting 'expert' to the school. Very often, even this is not followed up by any systematic investigation in the classroom and report-back by teachers. The principles upon which this model of teacher development is premised is that teachers develop by being 'filled up' with knowledge as provided by an external source.

These days, teacher development is widely understood to be something very different: it is something that happens within the classroom and within oneself. It is often initiated by teachers themselves, and the role of school-based support is to help channel these energies in directions that will be valuable and meaningful to the teachers concerned.

### The trainee trainer

It used to be the case – and still is in many places – that people became trainers by virtue of being experienced teachers. A common scenario is that a teacher moves 'up' into training as a career step or as a promotion. It is only recently that people have begun to realise that there is an important place for the *formal and systematic preparation* of trainers, as much as there is for the preparation of teachers (Wajnryb 1989). (In a way, this parallels the misinformed belief that the only prerequisite for teachers of English was a proficiency in the language.)

At the very least, trainer training involves two groups of people: experienced teachers wishing to prepare for the roles and responsibilities of training; and experienced trainers willing to systematise and pass on the fruits of their experience in training. It also usually involves other people, as a key element is 'field work' or practical experience in the classroom. This book may be used by those involved in trainer training to enhance and refine people's understanding of the classroom, specifically from the perspective of teacher preparation. For example, how do people learn to become teachers? Which teaching skills are 'trainable', that is, more skills-oriented, and which 'educable', that is, have more to do with knowledge and awareness? How can classroom observation be used in the training of teachers?

# 3 Why a book on observation?

## Why observe?

When we teach, we are often so absorbed in the purpose, procedure and logistics of our lesson that we are not able to observe processes of learning and interaction as they occur through the lesson. Being an observer in the classroom, rather than the teacher, *releases* us from these concerns and affords us the freedom to look at the lesson from a range of different perspectives outside that of the actual lesson plan of the teacher.

For the trainee teacher, this freedom is particularly important. In a way, this stage in training is akin to the 'silent phase' of a beginning language learner who listens, looks, observes, considers, analyses, reflects, but, significantly, is not required to produce (Dulay, Burt and Krashen 1982). Communication of this kind gives the learner a very particular role: they listen, read, are exposed to the target language but do not have to respond. Communication is one-way: directed *to*, not generated *from* the learner.

A 'silent phase' can influence learning. If we consider that the pressure to produce something channels all energies in one direction (performance), then the removal of this pressure releases a certain freedom: freedom to observe, absorb and reflect. A trainee teacher with the freedom to observe teaching is allowed time and space to become familiar with the culture of the classroom – its agenda of customs, rituals, expectations, patterns and mores – before having to try on any active aspects of the teacher's role (Wajnryb 1991). This book's observation tasks will structure and guide the silent phase of the trainee teacher's course of study.

Developing the skill of observing serves a dual purpose: it helps teachers gain a better understanding of their own teaching, while at the same time refines their ability to observe, analyse and interpret, an ability which can also be used to improve their own teaching. It is an underlying premise of this book that the development of the skills of observing is integral to the processes of professional decision-making in which teachers are constantly involved.

## What are observation tasks?

An observation task is a focussed activity to work on while observing a lesson in progress. It focusses on one or a small number of aspects of teaching or learning and requires the observer to collect data or information from the actual lesson, such as the language a teacher uses when giving instructions, or the patterns of interaction that emerge in a lesson. An observer may watch a lesson alone or with others; a number of observers may watch different lessons for the same reason, or in the case of a videoed or demonstration lesson, many observers may be involved simultaneously. The data collected may later be collated for purposes of analysis and interpretation.

See Section 4 (pages 16–17) on how the tasks are organised.

## Why tasks?

Because such a lot happens in the language learning classroom there is a lot to observe: teaching behaviour and learning behaviour, patterns of interaction, different learning styles, concentration spans, patterns of group dynamics, to name some. Sometimes what is happening is very overt, such as when a student asks a question and a teacher responds directly. Sometimes it is far more covert, such as when one student generalises from another's utterance and echoes an error. Often the connection between cause and effect is not immediately visible or retrievable.

Using an observation task helps the observer in two important ways:

1. It limits the scope of what one is observing and allows one to focus on one or two particular aspects, such as listening only to a certain type of question, or charting one student's concentration for a ten-minute time span, or recording non-verbal signals.
2. It provides a convenient means of collecting data that frees the observer from forming an opinion or making an on-the-spot evaluation during the lesson. The judgemental and interpretive side comes later, after the lesson, and will be based on the complete data that has been collected.

The tasks in this book are designed to give teachers:

- a 'way in' to discovering the classroom from a perspective other than that of the person actually teaching;
- a way of observing that provides both focus and clarity;
- a means of collecting classroom-based data and information about teaching;
- a meta-language: a language to talk about classrooms and the various processes related to teaching and learning;
- a raised awareness of classroom realities and a reservoir of information and experience that will serve them in discussing and reflecting on the classroom;
- a greater understanding of teaching and learning to enable their own classroom decision-making to be more informed and systematic;
- increased skill in interpreting and understanding data;
- an understanding of the relationship between theory and practice and a means of forging personally meaningful links between theoretical

knowledge about teaching and experience of the classroom. Sometimes this involves the top-down application of theory to the classroom; more often perhaps, it is the bottom-up recognition of theory emanating from practice (Lindstromberg 1990);

— a means towards building relationships with colleagues based on mutual respect and support;

— a respect for the classroom as the laboratory of language learning; a respect for data-driven, principled approaches to teaching; a healthy scepticism about unsupported claims.

## A theoretical framework

*Classroom Observation Tasks* offers practical materials to help make observation a learning tool by which teachers may learn and develop. Underlying these materials there is a theoretical framework, which might best be expressed as a number of guiding principles or tenets. These are detailed below under five headings:

1. A model of teacher development
2. The nature of help
3. The importance of the classroom
4. The 'trainability' of observation skills
5. The importance of task-based experience.

### 1 A MODEL OF TEACHER DEVELOPMENT

The model that guides the thinking and design of tasks in this book is that of *the reflective practitioner* (Schön 1983; Richards and Nunan 1990; Bartlett 1990), that is, a teacher who is discovering more about their own teaching by seeking to understand the processes of teaching and learning in their own and others' classrooms. This model has a number of key features which are worthy of description.

a) The model is built on an 'asset' rather than a 'deficit' premise: teachers bring to their own development a whole host of skills and experiences that will serve them. Likewise, the process of learning is an active, not a passive one: the teacher is actively reflecting and exploring, not, as it were, 'being developed' by someone else whose job might be to provide assessment and answers (Richards 1989).

b) Related to this concept of active engagement, is the concept of *learning as the construction of personal meaning*. In this view of learning, the teacher does not learn solely by acquiring new information or knowledge about teaching (such as new procedures or techniques), but through thinking about new ideas in the light of past experience, fitting new ideas into her or his thinking, and reappraising old assumptions in the light of new information. New information is therefore absorbed in a way that is creative, dynamic and personal and that will mean something different to each person receiving the information. The way a teacher learns, therefore, cannot be pre-ordained by the trainer. Freeman (1989) argues that in order to be effective, instruction has to offer the trainee 'the opportunity to engage with the material on an individual basis and assess [herself/himself] as a learner in the process' (Freeman 1989).

c) Following on from this notion of the personal construction of meaning is the point that teachers themselves are the primary *initiators* of their own development. The spirit of inquiry, the wish to reflect on one's own teaching, perhaps to explore other paths, comes from within the practitioner; it cannot be imposed from outside and then measured by some objective assessment tool. Likewise, the teacher is the one to determine and define their own end-point or expected outcome. Essentially all adult learning is voluntary; the motivation that steers and nourishes learning comes from within the learner, in our case, the teacher-learner.

d) The broad goals, therefore, of teacher education, must respect the agenda of the individual and must aim towards *teacher autonomy*, not dependence. By the very nature, therefore, of this model of teacher development, teacher educators cannot offer formulaic, top-down prescriptions. Not only do these tend to close off the pathways to autonomy for the teacher, as well as invest responsibility for change in the educator (instead of shifting it to the teacher), but they simply cannot provide answers for anything other than low-inference – readily learnable – skills (Richards 1990).

The more we have discovered about the classroom, the more we have come to respect the fact that the preparation of teachers involves teaching both low-inference skills, such as giving instructions or eliciting language, as well as higher-level decision-making (e.g. skills, such as interpreting learner error as 'local' or 'global', or knowing when and when not to correct). The latter are less readily learnable, being more abstract, more conceptual and more complex. Richards (1990) perceives this as a dilemma that is a challenge to teacher educators: how to deal with the fact that the aggregation of low-inference teaching skills does not necessarily result in good teaching. He calls for an approach to teacher training that accommodates both holistic and atomistic approaches, what he calls the macro- and micro-perspectives.

This book aims to follow this model of teacher development, and through the tasks to guide the teacher to observe, reflect on their observation, and take control of their own learning.

## 2 THE NATURE OF HELP

The second premise that underpins this book has to do with the nature of help, as the relationship between teacher trainer/developer and teacher is most often perceived as a helping one.

As already stated, it is inappropriate to see the role of teacher as deficient, passive and subordinate and trainer/developer as all-knowing, active and interventionist. This more traditional role relationship exists in many contexts. Conventionally the beginning teacher, and certainly the trainee, is the recipient of the wisdom of classroom 'veteran' practitioners. In other contexts, it may be that the teacher is on the receiving end of the latest findings of research into teaching and learning. Either way, we have an information transfer that is one-way.

Discussing the role relationship inevitably gives rise to questions about 'the nature of help'. Earlier I mentioned that providing formulaic answers, top-down, tends to give the responsibility for change to the educator, not the teacher and that this closes off pathways to autonomy. It does so by encouraging in the developing teacher a certain 'learned helplessness' (Abramson, Seligman and Teasdale 1978).

Fanselow (1990:183) sees 'helpful prescriptions' as 'stop[ping] exploration, since the receiver as someone in an inferior position being given orders by someone in a superior position, may easily develop the "ours is not to wonder why" syndrome'. Trainers/educators need to become more aware of the options available to them in interacting with trainees and teachers.

Providing people with pre-fabricated parcels of information is, as Freire (1970) has suggested, essentially oppressive, for it fails to take into account the fact that learning involves the personalised construction of meaning. Indeed, it may be that there is a certain contradiction in the role of the learner and the helper which has to be overcome if the learning process is to be successful.

In the place of the more traditional role of 'helper' and 'recipient', we are seeking a role relationship that is *collaborative and consultative*. The teacher is considered a co-investigator or co-explorer in the language classroom. The initiation for action and spirit of inquiry comes from the teacher. The role of the helper is to facilitate and guide learning, perhaps assist, where asked, in the identification of priorities or the provision of learning resources; essentially to respond rather than to initiate or steer.

An important part of this response from the helper assumes the capacity to accommodate and respect the learning style of the teacher in question. Just as, increasingly, language teachers are becoming sensitive to the need to recognise and accommodate the learning styles of language learners, so too teacher educators must be sensitive to the learning styles of teachers. Gebhard (1990) describes various choices of styles. The educator needs to choose wisely and judiciously, ever aware of how damaging prescriptiveness can be.

The collaborative relationship is not always easy to achieve. Sometimes this is because helpers are unwilling to let go of their traditionally dominant role. Sometimes, too, teachers are unprepared for taking on a more assertive and independent role as learners. For some there is a certain comfort in the very constraints of dependence. For many, previous educational contexts tend to set up expectations (albeit often subconscious) about how learning 'should happen'. If teacher educators have been reluctant to acknowledge different learning styles this is perhaps because the entire concept of learning styles is unknown to many teachers.

The collaborative model is consistent, too, with principles of mainstream adult education where a key feature is the voluntary nature of the learning experience. The overriding principle is that the learner needs to *own* responsibility for the learning processes and outcomes.

The discovery-oriented and inquiry-based spirit of this book aims to set in motion a means of teacher development where the initiation and motivation are essentially 'bottom-up'. Observing others teaching for the purpose of professional self-growth sidesteps, quite neatly, the traditional power bases of people involved in teacher education. Teachers can make their own choices about what they wish to focus on rather than subscribing to externally-imposed decisions about the direction of their professional development.

Fanselow (1990:184) has a beautiful image of classroom observation as a journey towards discovery and self-knowledge. It places the teacher-as-learner at the centre of the experience and has little scope for external help in the conventional, dependent sense:

> Here I am with my lens to look at you and your actions. But as I look at you with my lens, I consider you a mirror. I hope to see myself in you and through my teaching. When I see myself, I find it hard to get distance from my teaching. I hear my voice, I see my face and clothes, and fail to see my teaching. Seeing you allows me to see myself differently and to explore the variables we both use.

In analysing the nature of help in the process of teacher development, it is valuable to bear in mind what the long-term aims of this development might be. Essentially the process is one that should foster the growth of independent teachers capable of making independent decisions. In Richards's view (1990) it is the high-inference skills that allow teachers to make these decisions and to respond effectively to the needs and demands in their classroom, many of which cannot be predicted in the here and now.

In the consideration of the short- and long-term goals of professional development, Prabhu's concepts of 'equipping' and 'enabling' (1987a) may be pertinent. 'Equipping' is concerned with providing the teacher with the skills and knowledge needed for immediate use; 'enabling' is concerned with developing the teacher's ability to meet and respond to future professional demands. Linking Prabhu's metaphor, then, to Richards's hierarchy of teacher skills (1990), if 'equipping' is an apt metaphor for the low-inference teacher skills, 'enabling' serves comparably for the high-inference ones. Certainly, investigating, exploring and seeking to understand classroom processes, as intended by this book, is an important step in the long-term 'enabling' process to which we are committed.

### 3 THE IMPORTANCE OF THE CLASSROOM

The third tenet that underlies this book is the primacy of the classroom in any programme of teacher preparation or development. The view taken is that the teacher – not the trainer or developer – is the principal agent of change in language teaching and that the natural habitat of the teacher, of course, is the classroom: this is where their experience is based and this is where their growth will take effect. The language classroom is the primary *source of information* out of which teachers will develop their own personal philosophy of what makes effective teaching and learning. It is also the domain where they will find out about their professional roles and responsibilities. The tasks in this book are firmly anchored in the classroom context and aim to make the classroom a familiar, comfortable and secure environment for teachers. It is here that they will derive both the experience and the theory that will be personally meaningful for them.

### 4 THE 'TRAINABILITY' OF OBSERVATION SKILLS

A major assumption of this book is that the skills of observation are not wholly intuitive but can be learnt. This book seeks to structure and focus this learning process through a set of focussed classroom tasks which engage the observer. By broadening, deepening and refining the powers of observation, these tasks are designed to guide the growth of the teacher's critical abilities. This is seen as firm ground on which to build the skills of analysis, interpretation and self-evaluation. These skills are clearly linked with teachers' ability to analyse what goes on in their *own* classrooms so as to help them make better professional decisions.

Different people, of course, bring different backgrounds with them to the classroom. We are all, from this point of view, the sum total of our life already led. So a teacher brings to the language classroom many expectations derived from teaching and learning experiences both recent and past. Some researchers claim that much of one's teaching is derived from one's own experience of learning, and that these 'ghosts behind the blackboard' must be identified if they are to be exorcised (see Weintraub 1989; Tyler 1989).

Confronting hidden assumptions as well as verbalising teachers' expectations is part of what happens when one begins to take on the skills of observation. A teacher, for example, may assume that her or his manner of organising group work, or handling correction is successful and effective; she or he may confront these unstated assumptions by observing other teachers doing similar or different things in the classroom. This is consistent with observation as a 'mirroring' tool, as described by Fanselow (1990).

Very often the crucial thrust of teacher development is asking questions of behaviours that are (or have become) ritualised (Maingay 1988). Maingay defines ritual teaching behaviour as

> teaching that is unthinking; that is . . . divorced from the principles that lie behind it; it is . . . either purely imitative or . . . set into patterns that no longer reveal awareness on the teacher's part of why he or she should be teaching in that particular way. (1988:118–19)

This is contrasted with 'principled teaching behaviour' which is defined as 'teaching that is informed by principles that the teacher is aware of' (*ibid.*:119).

Very often these rituals are learned at the pre-service level, when, in short intensive courses, the combination of pressure of time and pressure to perform sometimes compels trainees to adopt short-cut learning strategies such as learning a ritual without fully understanding its rationale (Gower 1988). As well, there is the urgency to 'perform' before much exposure to input has occurred. Rituals are comforting in the sense that they provide a certain security at a time when a teacher is looking for survival skills and strategies. The danger is that the principles behind the techniques are not understood, resulting in techniques being enacted and re-enacted as lip-service ritual.

The other advantage of rituals is that they release the teacher to think about other aspects of the lesson. Once the strategy is mastered at the level of ritual, a certain freedom is generated to enable the teacher to consider elements outside of immediate survival. The teacher who has a repertoire of reflex behaviours or rituals, in a sense is not burdened by the myriad of little, apparently trivial decisions that are called for in the classroom.

It often happens, too, that what was once learned as principled, thinking behaviour 'degenerates' over time into ritual through the force of habit and repetition and over-use.

Thus while some ritual is inevitable, there is still a need for re-appraisal to prevent rituals becoming fossilised into pre-fabricated patterns of teaching behaviour. A key means towards this end is peer observation: 'It is . . . one of the observer's roles to alert a teacher to such behaviour and its consequences and to make him or her aware of the need for regular examination of what has become ritual' (*ibid.*:127).

One reason why trainer training serves as an excellent means of staff development is that it compels teachers to reflect on and re-vitalise their thinking about teaching, and thereby inevitably subject their own teaching behaviour to scrutiny.

The process of reflecting and re-appraising is the stuff of which teacher development is made. The willingness to reflect and confront hardened assumptions must, of course, be totally voluntary and must come from within, not be imposed from outside. It will only happen in a risk-free and supportive professional context. One challenge of the teacher educator is to ensure that the context in which self-discovery takes place is a safe one.

### 5 THE IMPORTANCE OF TASK-BASED EXPERIENCE

The fifth premise of this book is the role of experience in the preparation and development of teachers. Few today would argue with the notion that people learn best when they are actively engaged in the learning process. Active engagement can take many forms: doing, thinking, reacting, absorbing, observing, reflecting, preparing, considering, applying, analysing, listing, selecting, prioritising, ranking, interpreting, completing, comparing, re-arranging, evaluation – among others (Ellis 1990).

*The task* is viewed in this book as a key way of achieving active involvement. A number of features of task-based learning deserve mention:

a) Tasks allow the observation process to become *personalised*. The task allows the observer the opportunity to engage with the experience on an individual basis. This 'injection of self' into the process allows the observer to reflect and explore both their own teaching as well as the teaching being observed (Freeman 1989).

b) Tasks allow learning to be *generative*: that is, 'the instructional process [is] productive in a mathematical sense such that it teaches both content and a way of thinking which can continue to generate solutions beyond that specific context . . .' (Freeman 1989). This is important because it means that the teacher's development is becoming autonomous: 'he [*sic*] can then apply the way of thinking to derive other content independent of the trainer or instructional setting' (Freeman 1989:37).

c) The task is also essentially *inquiry-based, discovery-oriented, inductive* and potentially *problem-solving*. As such, it allows teachers to come to their own understanding of the classroom based on their own experience instead of giving them pre-packaged solutions. Instead then of directing answers, a task leads logically to discussion and debate among teachers.

d) Lastly, the task allows teachers to build up experience and understanding that will serve them as a *resource base* for their own teaching and classroom decision-making. This view of teacher development is one that sees development as an ongoing process initiated by the teacher's own inquiries and nourished by the experiences gained by that teacher in seeking solutions to classroom problems. Thus even teacher trainees with no teaching experience are provided, through a programme of peer observation in their practicum, with a personally meaningful data base.

## 4 How the tasks are organised

The tasks in this book are grouped into the following sections.

1. The learner
2. Language
3. Learning
4. The lesson
5. Teaching skills and strategies
6. Classroom management
7. Materials and resources

Each task deals with a facet of the central focus: for example, in 4. *The lesson*, some of the areas covered are types of activities in a lesson; changes of direction within a lesson; lesson signposting; ways of opening and closing a lesson, and negotiation in lesson breakdowns.

This categorisation of tasks into different focuses is employed to create an ordered and easily usable book. It is not meant to suggest that different aspects of classroom behaviour are to be rigidly confined to one focus and nowhere else. Often, in fact, a particular aspect of the classroom might be approached from two (or more) different angles and therefore may fall into more than one focus area. Some examples open many doors: a topic like learner error may be approached from the perspective of 'language' or 'teaching skills and strategies' or 'the learner' or 'classroom management'. Constraints of space have prevented us from approaching each topic exhaustively from every potential perspective.

It is not expected that the tasks will be selected in the order in which they appear, but rather that the selection will be made on the basis of teachers' needs and concerns.

An alphabetical *Task index* at the back of the book allows you to find a task directly, without first consulting the focus section.

## How each task is organised

Different people will approach the tasks for different reasons and with different objectives in mind. The tasks themselves, however, follow a standard format.

At the beginning you will find a brief *background* statement about the particular facet of classroom behaviour that is to be focussed on. This is followed by a statement of *objective*. Here you will find out what the purpose of the task is, and what end-result is intended. Then there is a section on *procedure*. This consists of three phases: before the lesson, during the lesson, and after the lesson.

Typically, the instructions for the *Before the lesson* phase deal with some preliminary activity such as making contact with the teacher, reading through the lesson plan, or making yourself familiar with an aspect of the lesson. Sometimes, you may be asked to prepare in some way, such as writing instructions to lead into an activity. (During the lesson you might then compare your own scripted instructions with those of the teacher during the lesson.)

*During the lesson* the task will require you to collect data and a grid or chart is provided to enable you to do this with ease. Where possible an example is given so that the idea will be quite clear.

*After the lesson* is the time for discussion, analysis and interpretation. Once again, how this is conducted will, to a large extent, depend on the learning/teaching context in which you find yourself. There is, of course, no requirement to answer all the questions or to give them all the same degree of attention.

The tasks are uniform in format but the *emphasis* within this format varies. Sometimes, the emphasis is on the data collection process. At other times it is on the consideration of issues leading into the task; in other cases, again, the emphasis is on the analysis and discussion in the *After the lesson* phase.

More specific guidance in using the tasks is found in the next section: *How to use the tasks*.

## 5   How to use the tasks

This section offers guidance to the various groups of people to whom this book is addressed. These groups and the contexts they work in were identified in Section 2 (pages 2–6).

Part 1: Introduction

## The context of teacher development

THE TEACHER

A few typical scenarios in which the teacher might use the tasks in this book are outlined below.

SCENARIO 1

You are keen to explore your teaching and generally wish to find out more about how you teach. You invite a colleague into your classroom and ask them to collect data about a particular aspect of your teaching, for example, the way you use questions, the spread of your attention through the class, your use of the board, or the patterns of interaction through your lesson. Your observer will, at an agreed time, observe you in the classroom from the agreed perspective. Following this, the two of you will confer and the data collected will serve you to discover more about what happens when you teach.

In this situation it is important that the teacher being observed defines exactly what will be observed so that she or he retains ownership of the experience.

SCENARIO 2

A group of teachers wishes to initiate and engage in a programme of action research investigating a particular form of classroom activity, for example, patterns of interaction in multilingual classes; the spread of teacher attention in co-educational classes; the effect of question-type on student response. You each choose to observe a number of lessons by different teachers using an agreed means of collecting and recording data. Apart from the actual observation of lessons, such a programme requires preliminary meetings to establish commonalities of purpose, allocate tasks, set guidelines and time frames; and follow-up meetings to de-brief, pool data, analyse and interpret findings. It may be that as a group you will look to someone else outside the group – perhaps someone involved in school-based teacher support – to help manage and steer the working group.

SCENARIO 3

Two teachers decide to observe each other to look at a particular aspect of their teaching. This again would lead to a post-lesson conference where the teachers would exchange opinions and ideas on the areas of concern.

These three scenarios may indicate the range of different purposes that exist for observing teaching. However some guiding principles are common to all and they are worth bearing in mind.

## SOME GUIDING PRINCIPLES FOR OBSERVING

1. Observers need to maintain a sensitive awareness of the potential for vulnerability that inevitably accompanies any observation of teaching. When a teacher opens the classroom door and extends a welcome to a visitor, a basic trust in motive and professional ethic accompanies that welcome. This must be respected.
2. The presence of a visitor inevitably affects the classroom dynamics. Observers should take every care to minimise the intrusion and allow for this factor in drawing conclusions from the data.
3. Observers need to realise that the samples of data brought from the classroom are inevitably limited, and that sweeping generalisations should be avoided. We need to talk about *what happened in the lesson* (a particular observed lesson), and refrain from making the unwarranted leap to *what happens in lessons* (generally).
4. Sometimes the task will entail some preliminary collaboration and co-operation with the teacher who is going to be observed. For example, Task 5.4, *Giving instructions*, you will need to see in advance the lesson plan that the teacher intends to follow. At other times, it will be necessary *not* to alert the teacher to the central point of the observation for fear of 'contaminating' the data. For example, if a teacher knows in advance that their 'echoes' are going to be recorded, or that their questions will be under scrutiny, this knowledge may affect their language through the lesson. This element of concealment has to do with research method, and care should be taken that such matters are handled with discretion and professionalism.
5. While the above precautions are necessary for methodological validity, it is as important on the human and professional side, to be sure to share with the observed teacher any follow-up discussions about the lesson. The question of 'ownership of the experience' is an important one and requires sensitive awareness. We need to remember that the experience has to be meaningful, rewarding and non-threatening to all involved: teacher, observer, learners, colleagues, tutors, etc.

## Part 1: Introduction

### *The context of pre-service training*

#### THE TRAINEE TEACHER

How you use the book will, to a large extent, depend on your training/learning/teaching contexts. Here are a number of possible scenarios.

#### SCENARIO 1

As a forerunner to the practical module of your training course, you are asked to observe a number of lessons over a certain period of time. This 'silent phase' or warm-up period, is designed to introduce you to the culture of the classroom in a gentle and non-threatening manner so that you will begin to feel comfortable in what is to become your natural habitat! This book will give you the structure and guidance that you need to help make sense of what initially may be very unfamiliar terrain. Your trainers or support teachers will guide you in the selection and management of tasks.

You may follow up these observations in a number of ways: through a meeting with the observed teacher; a meeting of co-trainees pooling experiences and data; or in a tutorial group steered by a trainer.

#### SCENARIO 2

The observation tasks are closely integrated into your training programme and a trainer or co-operating teacher selects a particular theme or skill for a set of lessons to be observed.

#### SCENARIO 3

The choice of task is left open to you or to a group of trainees working in a micro-group, a teaching practice group or a tutorial context. You will need to consider which aspect of the classroom you would like to know more about.

The inspiration for the task you choose may derive from a lecture or workshop in which you have participated. For example, in conjunction with a session on eliciting skills, you may wish to observe a lesson for this purpose. In this case you will find 'eliciting' in *5. Teaching skills and strategies*, or directly (under E) in the Task index at the back of the book.

It may be that after the observation trainees then meet for a tutorial where they discuss the data they have collected.

SCENARIO 4

As a consequence of having your own teaching observed, you have become more aware of, say, the potential uses of classroom space and teacher movement. So you seek out a task related to this area (or you ask a trainer to recommend one for you). Then you observe a more experienced teacher and collect data about this particular aspect of teaching.

THE TEACHER TRAINER

PERFORMANCE AND OBSERVATION

An important component of pre-service courses for language teachers is the teaching practice that trainees do either in individual lessons or sometimes in shared classes. In the teaching practice phase, the focus is often on the teacher's performance. This book takes the focus away from the performance element of teaching and places it on the observation of teaching. The importance of observation at the pre-service stage has been discussed in Section 3 (see page 7). The point has been made that a period of guided observation will prepare teachers for the kinds of decision-making that they will engage in throughout their careers.

There are a few key elements in the observation component of a training course that you, the trainer, might wish to bear in mind:

1. Trainees need time to adjust to, and become familiar and comfortable with the language learning classroom. A period of observation can help here. This may take the form of peer observation, observation of more experienced teachers, or more structured and guided observation, such as that afforded by the use of pre-recorded videos in training sessions.
2. Training should not be limited to making trainees competent at a survival level, but should prepare them for the sorts of processes that they will encounter as teachers. This means encouraging a spirit of inquiry about the bases of effective teaching.
3. The value of a non-prescriptive approach to teacher training was discussed in Section 3 (see pages 11–13). This book offers a less prescriptive approach to training. The questions and tasks in the *After the lesson* section call for teachers and trainers alike to reflect on their experiences as observers and teachers and to draw and discuss inferences from these experiences.
4. Observation of classes can be linked to other channels of learning that occur in a course, e.g. lectures, tutorials or workshops. How this is actually programmed may vary from one context to another.

# Part 1: Introduction

In using this book trainers are reminded that 'the teacher as reflective practitioner' is the ultimate autonomous goal of the educative process. With this model of teacher growth in mind, you, the trainer, are encouraged to:

- remain sensitive to how people learn, and how people learn to become teachers;
- consider your role as one facilitating growth rather than giving information, answers or solutions;
- avoid being judgemental in a way that reinforces the power invested in your position and the powerlessness of the trainee.

## THE TRAINER'S ROLE

The trainer's role will make an impact on the learning process at a number of stages in the process of working with this book.

1. *Selecting tasks* should, as much as possible, be considered a shared and consultative process between trainer and trainee. As trainer, consider the trainee's individual strengths, weaknesses, interests and learning style; remember, too, that experiences initiated by trainees are likely to be the ones most valued by them; be careful to link up the tasks selected to other channels of learning in the course. These inter-connections within the curriculum should be made apparent to the trainee and not assumed to be shared knowledge.
2. The *pre-observation stage* is an important time for an airing of interests and concerns where, once again, the active involvement of the trainee at the decision-making level will best guarantee their motivation and commitment.
3. Ground rules for the *actual observation* need to be negotiated and maintained. Trainers need to bear in mind that the experience belongs to the trainee who must enter and leave the experience with 'a sense of ownership'. Equally, trainers need to be aware that the presence of observers affects a learning community in both visible and imperceptible ways. You have to be careful to avoid setting up negative or hostile currents in the classroom.
4. *Post-lesson* consultations, tutorials and discussions provide an important and valuable area where you, the trainer, can furnish many opportunities for trainees to reflect on the factors that influence decision-making in the classroom. Earlier, mention was made of the need to make pre-service training more 'developmental' in the sense of alerting and sensitising trainees to the sorts of decisions and processes that they will be engaging in as teachers. In the discussion component of the observation process – whether this precedes or

follows the actual observation – trainers have an opportunity to cross the line from 'training' to 'developing'. This may be achieved by encouraging and steering the sorts of discussions that take trainees and trainers alike beyond the surface level of visible technique – 'skills and competencies' – to the discovery of 'the working rules that effective teachers use' (Richards 1990:15).

POSSIBLE SCENARIOS

Here are some suggestions of ways in which this book might be used in training.

1. Set up a programme of observation tasks from the book for trainees to guide the 'silent phase' of their introduction to the classroom.
2. Set up a number of observation tasks that are closely integrated with other channels of learning on the course. For example, the topic area of *classroom management* may be approached via a number of points of entry: lecture; observation of teaching; being observed by a peer teacher; tutorials devoted to discussing data collected during observations.
3. Set an observation task on a one-to-one basis or small group level in response to the individual or collective needs of a particular trainee or group of trainees.
4. Using a section of a pre-recorded videoed lesson, set tasks as a group exercise to be done in class.
5. Using the suggested discussion topics in the *After the lesson* section of the tasks, focus the agenda of a tutorial or workshop on a set of pre-set questions. This may or may not be based on a series of observations completed by all the participants in the tutorial.

In such ways as these, observation tasks can be meaningfully and successfully integrated into a training programme.

## The context of school-based teacher support

With the increasing acceptance of the principle of professional development, and with the 'reflective practitioner' being increasingly recognised as a valid developmental model (Bartlett 1990), many schools have begun to provide support services for their teaching staff. This is not the place to describe the various systems in place, but rather to point to some of the underlying principles that they share. These include:

- teachers in the post-initial training stage of their career need an ongoing diet of reflection and stimulation;
- initiation for this must necessarily stem from teachers themselves;
- a supportive environment is one in which observation is linked with

growth, not assessment, probation or employment;
– support personnel are in a facilitative role, resourcing the self-discovery process that teachers undertake.

An awareness of these issues should go a long way to ensure that the tasks here are used to structure and enhance the growth of teachers. Here are a few scenarios in which support personnel may use classroom observation as an important tool in supporting professional development in their school.

### SCENARIO 1

A teacher is worried about a particular aspect of their teaching, and approaches you about it. You confer with the teacher in order to explore the matter in greater depth. What is the worry? What actually happens? Why does the teacher think it happens? Your aim here is to encourage the teacher to talk about the problem and begin to speculate on it in broader terms. You then suggest a number of courses of action: the teacher might observe a few teachers' classrooms, using structured tasks, and collect some data from the observation in order to furnish a follow-up discussion. Or the teacher might invite an observer into their own classroom to record aspects of the teaching using the task structure. This too would lead to another meeting in which you would encourage the teacher to draw inferences from the data collected and begin to understand better the what, whys and hows of the situation. It is always wise to confer with teachers so as to find out their preferred course – or combination of courses – of action.

### SCENARIO 2

You have become aware that there is a particular area of language teaching with which many teachers in the school need help. You plan a presentation and workshop on the subject but prefer to have participants arrive 'warm' and motivated. As a lead-up to the workshop, you set up a series of structured peer observations using particular tasks that relate to the area of interest that is the subject of your workshop. You hope to call on the data collected and together pool thoughts to interpret and discuss the findings. You hope that by using data and experiences that are personally meaningful participants will 'invest' in the learning and give it value. You also hope that the inquiry will not end here: you would see it as a sign of success if some of the teachers asked for your continued support as they pursue their inquiries further.

## The context of trainer training

Trainer training means the preparation of experienced teachers for the various roles and responsibilities of teacher training and teacher preparation. A number of considerations are worthy of mention and these pertain to the assumptions that *cannot* be made in the training of trainers:

1. We cannot assume a familiarity with the client: just as beginning teachers need to become aware of and familiar with 'the language learner', so beginning trainers need to become aware of and familiar with 'trainee teachers'.
2. We cannot assume that because they are experienced teachers, they necessarily remember or understand well the process of becoming a teacher.
3. We cannot assume that experienced teachers are necessarily consciously aware of many of the processes that co-occur in the classroom or that they have had opportunities to articulate their thoughts on these. They may therefore lack a meta-language – a language to talk about teaching and training.

Observation of trainee teachers is crucial to the preparation of trainers, for it is through observing that they may gradually become more familiar with trainees, more familiar with and articulate about the classroom and learning/teaching processes, and more conversant in ways of talking about classroom experiences.

This book can help to structure and focus the experience. Here are two scenarios:

### SCENARIO 1

A trainee trainer observes a teaching practice lesson given by a trainee teacher. Some data are collected from the lesson, using a particular task. In a follow-up tutorial or discussion, the trainee trainer seeks to identify in what way they might be able to facilitate learning by the trainee teacher in perhaps the short term (e.g. as preparation for the latter's next lesson) or in the longer term. Discussion focusses on how the authentic data can be used as an aid to learning by the trainee.

### SCENARIO 2

A trainee trainer is asked to prepare a session for a group of trainee teachers on an aspect of language teaching, for example, ways in which meanings of words can be conveyed. As a point of departure into researching this topic, the trainee trainer collects some authentic data about this particular aspect of teaching by observing a teacher (or trainee) and focussing on this aspect of teaching. This then becomes the springboard for the presentation, which may in turn encourage trainees to continue their understanding through peer observation on the same or a related topic.

## A word of caution

Teaching and learning are meant to converge in the classroom and very often they do. A key element in the various patterns of the classroom is the human factor – the individual teacher, learner, observer. Together, with and through each other, there is great potential for collaboration and learning.

Sensitivity is needed to issues such as cross-cultural factors, territoriality, 'face' and vulnerability. When we allow in a visitor to an established learning community or when we ourselves enter the formerly closed territory of a group of learners, we have an effect on the dynamics and the ambience of the group.

Many questions are precipitated but not necessarily asked: Do the students know who the observers are and why they are there? Is the teacher secretly harbouring anxieties about being judged? Do the students, for example, suspect that the teacher's teaching is under suspicion? Will this detract from their respect for the teacher? Do the students think they are being (secretly) tested? These questions and many like them testify to the great bonds of trust that we invoke and place in jeopardy when we take on observation as a learning tool.

This does not mean that we should avoid it, but simply that we should not underestimate its fragility. Proper attention to sensitive and delicate areas like these can help make the experience of observation very worthwhile for all involved.

# Part Two   The tasks

## Introduction to the tasks

This section contains the classroom tasks. The organisation of the tasks and suggested guidelines for their use are outlined in Sections 4 and 5 of the Introduction.

Each task has a standard format that helps guide the user through the phases of the observation. Although different users may use the tasks for different purposes, the format has been standardised for clarity and continuity. Even though the observation may be initiated by the classroom teacher or by the observer, the tasks are addressed to the observing teacher to be consistent.

# 1 The learner

## 1.1 Attending to the learner

### BACKGROUND

A group of learners in a classroom with a teacher comprises a learning community. The human element – both verbal and non-verbal, visible and barely perceptible – shapes human interaction qualitatively and may perhaps furnish the key to what happens (the processes) and what eventuates (the outcomes).

Approaches to language teaching that draw on an understanding of humanistic psychology highlight the importance to learning of the affective learning environment. It has been said that one can't teach a language – the best one can do is to make the conditions right for others to learn. Part of these 'right conditions' involves how the teacher relates to – or attends to – the learners.

### TASK OBJECTIVE

In this lesson you will be paying very close attention to the teacher's attending behaviour towards the learners – that is, the way a teacher acknowledges, through verbal or non-verbal means, the presence, contribution, and needs of individual learners. There are many facets to attending behaviour. One of the more obvious of these is using students' names. Others are eye contact, touch, facial expression, etc.

### PROCEDURE

*BEFORE THE LESSON*

1. Arrange to observe a lesson.
2. Make yourself familiar with the sample diagram opposite. Be aware that you will probably have to modify it or draw up a new one to reflect the seating arrangements in the classroom. Each box should represent a student. You may want to go into the room early to start doing this, or you may be able to ask the teacher to prepare one for you.

*DURING THE LESSON*

1. Make sure you are seated in a position where you are able to observe when and how the teacher attends to individuals – by names, gesture, stance, facing them or not, eye contact, verbal prompts, etc.
2. For a portion of the lesson (decide yourself how much of the lesson you wish to devote to the collection of data), keep a record of every time the teacher attends: mark the appropriate box (perhaps with a dot) each time the teacher attends to a particular person.
3. As the teacher's use of names allows you to identify the learners, name each box on your diagram.
4. As far as you are able, try also to make a note (see list below) of the actual attending strategy used by the teacher. Some likely ones are listed. You may like to add others as you observe. It may help to use an abbreviation code. Sometimes strategies overlap or are combined: you may like to indicate this, for example, smile/eye contact (overlap); name + smile (combined).
5. Note on your diagram, too, whether the students are male or female and any other distinguishing characteristics, such as a difference in age, nationality.
6. You may wish to record some field notes on student response to the teacher's attending strategies, for example, when the teacher looks at a student to discourage talking, or to encourage a response.

## Seating arrangements

| Wu<br>F ● | M | F | Matilda<br>● ● F | M | M | F |
|---|---|---|---|---|---|---|
| M | | | | | | F |
| M | | | | | | Julio<br>M<br>●●●● |
| F | | | | | | F |
| F | | | | | | F |
| M | | | | | | M |

## Attending strategies

name (N)

nod (↓)

smile (⌣)

eye contact (⊙)

reprimanding look (⌒)

touch (T)

*AFTER THE LESSON*

1. Share the data with the classroom teacher and together consider your impressions.
2. Do any patterns emerge? Were some students named or attended to more often than others?
3. Is there any 'pattern within the pattern'? For example:

   - Is the sex of the student relevant to the distribution of teacher attention?
   - Does the seating arrangement lend itself to a particular spread of teacher attention?
   - Is there a category of student that is attended to more or less than the others?
   - Do weaker or stronger students tend to 'disappear'?
   - What general conclusions can you draw about attending behaviour?

4. Focus on the use of names. Try to recall how these were used: for what purpose and to what effect? Speaking generally, what purposes can be served through the use of names? What means can teachers use to help them recall names?
5. Now consider the range of attending strategies used by the teacher. What others are possible? What comment would you make on a teacher's having a range of attending strategies? Are these conscious or subconscious behaviours in a teacher? Perhaps share the list of attending strategies noted with the classroom teacher and discuss whether these were consciously used.
6. Did you happen to notice anything about the students' own attending behaviours towards other students? How important is this? What might the teacher's role be in this regard? Is this in any way connected to their language learning agenda?

## REFLECTION

Using the lesson as a mirror of your own attending skills, what comment can you make about your own teaching behaviour? What have you learned from this observation that you could apply to your own teaching?

## 1.2 Learner motivation

### BACKGROUND

What motivates learners? Why do people sometimes put so much effort and energy into learning another language? In trying to understand the motivation that drives language learning, major studies have in the past tended to divide motivation into two broad categories: instrumental and integrative (see, for example, Gardner and Lambert 1972).

Broadly, *instrumental* motivation refers to wanting to learn a language because it will be useful for certain 'instrumental' and practical goals, such as getting a job, reading foreign newspapers or texts, passing an exam or obtaining a promotion. This category also includes more negative factors such as fear of failure. *Integrative* motivation, on the other hand, refers to wanting to learn a language for reasons of understanding, relating to or communicating with the people of the culture who speak it.

In the past, it was considered that learners with integrative motivation were more successful than learners with the 'lesser' drive of instrumental motivation. More recent studies (e.g. Giles and Byrne 1982) have cast doubt on this assumption. It is now believed that the categories of instrumental/integrative are not quite as distinct as may have been previously depicted: a learner's motivation may contain a blend of elements from both categories. It is also now believed that the former correlation between integrative–success and instrumental–less success is in fact quite facile and fails to reflect the true complexity of motivation.

What has emerged is that whatever the basis of the motivation of the learner, its level (high/low) has an impact on expected learner roles. Highly motivated learners are more likely to synchronise their roles willingly with the teacher's role; and are more likely to co-operate with the teacher in the various processes involved in classroom learning (Wright 1987).

### TASK OBJECTIVE

This task will encourage you to consider learners from the point of view of their individual motivation for learning.

### PROCEDURE

*BEFORE THE LESSON*

1. Arrange to observe a class of learners whom you know well. This ideally might be your own class being taught by someone else.

2. Make yourself familiar with the chart below.
3. Choose a range of about five students whom you consider you know well enough to comment on their motivation for learning. Consider their reasons for wanting to learn the language. Comment in the column marked *Motivation* whether you consider it to be high or low or otherwise make a relevant comment.

*DURING THE LESSON*

1. Consider these students' behaviour/role in class and the degree to which they synchronise and co-operate with the teacher. For example, consider a student's:

   — response to the teacher;
   — involvement in tasks;
   — willingness to ask when uncertain;
   — tolerance of other students, etc.

2. There is room in the far right column for any further comments. You may, for example, wish to consider whether the motivation might be described as instrumental, integrative or a blend of these.

| Student's name | Motivation | Learning behaviour | Comment |
|---|---|---|---|
|  |  |  |  |

1.2 Learner motivation

*AFTER THE LESSON*

1. Consider the data you have collected. Comment on any linkage between Columns 2 and 3.
2. As it is so easy to make assumptions, you may wish to confirm your understanding of the students' motivations by interviewing them.
3. How important is it that a teacher knows their students well enough to understand the various motivations for learning the language?

   What means/methods might a teacher deploy in order to obtain this information? Which of these strategies do you use in your own teaching situation?
4. We now recognise that the distinctions of integrative and instrumental motivation are not as broad and clear as was once believed. Nevertheless, the following task may be beneficial.

   Link the following factors to either integrative or instrumental motivation. Or, if you wish, create an alternative scheme of classification.

   — Low degree of ethnocentrism
   — Wanting to obtain work in the target language
   — Planning to use the language for travel
   — Cultural value attached to learning another language
   — Having a close relationship with someone who speaks the target language
   — A love of culture, travel and contact with other people
   — Needs related to current or future study or work
   — A wish to 'be more like' people who speak the target language

   You may like to add any other motivations that you are aware of through your contact with language learning situations.
5. Consider your own attempts to learn another language. How would you define your motivation? How successful were you? To what extent do you link your success rate with your motivation? Or, to what extent do you think your success or otherwise affected your motivation?

## REFLECTION

This task has involved you in actively considering various motivations that affect students in their learning a language. In what way might this experience affect you when you resume a teaching role with this (or another) group of students?

## 1.3 The learner as doer

### BACKGROUND

It is commonly recognised that active learning allows learning to be both more personal and more memorable and for these reasons, is more effective. Learners who are 'engaged' by the lesson – by the teacher, the materials, the tasks, the activities – are more likely to have that learning make an impact on them. Teachers, therefore, often incorporate tasks in their teaching that require learners to *do* something in the lesson, for example, with the language or with each other.

### TASK OBJECTIVE

The purpose of this observation is to allow you to become sensitive to the fact that 'learning by doing' embraces a large range of activities, and to analyse these activities as being *cognitive* (thinking), *affective* (feeling) and *physical*.

### PROCEDURE

*BEFORE THE LESSON*

1. Arrange to observe a lesson. Prepare yourself for the 'nature of doing' by considering the sorts of things that teachers typically ask students to do. For example, tasks may involve:

   – thinking;
   – feeling;
   – acting;
   – moving about;
   – prioritising, ranking, making judgements;
   – negotiating, interacting with others;
   – consulting other sources of information.

2. Make yourself familiar with the chart opposite.

*DURING THE LESSON*

1. Observe the lesson from the point of view of what the learners actually do.
2. Use the chart to help you collect data from the lesson. Note down:

   – what the learners do;
   – what this involves;
   – what you think the teacher's purpose is.

Add any comments in the far right column, for example, whether you would label the activity cognitive, affective, physical.

| What learners do | What this involves | Teacher's purpose | Comment |
|---|---|---|---|
| Grouping words according to meaning | - Referring to dictionary<br><br>- Consulting other students | -Teach reference skills<br><br>- Teach two layers of meaning: denotation and connotation | Cognitive |

## 1.3 The learner as doer

*AFTER THE LESSON*

1. Together with the classroom teacher, consider the balance of cognitive, affective and physical activities involved in the lesson. Discuss your views on this.
2. Considering the data you have collected, which activities in the lesson do you consider were the most valuable for the learners? Why were they valuable?
3. While we might, as teachers, encourage active involvement in the lesson, what happens when this planned learning style is incongruent or incompatible with a learner's own learning style? To what degree should a teacher compromise their preferred teaching methodology so as to cater for a learner's own preferred learning methodology?

## REFLECTION

Use this lesson as a mirror of your own teaching. What balance of activities does your teaching typically involve? Has your awareness of these factors altered in any way that may influence your approach?

## 1.4 Learner level

### BACKGROUND

The assumption underlying this task is that no one class is ever completely homogenous in terms of level. Even if we might say that on Day One of the course, a class *appears* homogenous, by the end of the first week, patterns and gradations of levels will have begun to appear.

The notion of level is itself a complex one, related to and influenced by other differences among learners. The more we discover about language learning the more we are confronted by the diversity of contingent factors: people learn in different ways, at different rates, with different styles and exposing different strategies. There are other cases of 'anomaly' too, such as the risk-avoiding, accuracy-oriented student who might *appear* to be a higher level than the rather garrulous, risk-taking fluency or communication-oriented student who is less perturbed by a display of error.

### TASK OBJECTIVE

The objective of this unit of observation is to recognise the overt signs of learner level as well as aspects of teaching that indicate that the teacher is accommodating learner level.

### PROCEDURE

*BEFORE THE LESSON*

1. Arrange to observe a class of mixed-level students.
2. Meet with the teacher and find out some of the learners' names and their respective levels. Have the teachers grade the learners in the class on a key, for example, 1 to 5, where 1 is near the lowest in the class, and 5 the highest.
3. Ask the teacher to have the students wear name labels as you will need to be able to recognise them.
4. Make yourself familiar with the chart opposite.

*DURING THE LESSON*

1. Using the chart to collect your data, look for overt evidence of the students' designated levels.
2. In the far right column, record the strategies used by the teacher to accommodate learner level.

| Student | Level | Signs of level | Teacher's strategies |
|---------|-------|----------------|----------------------|
| Miguel | 1 | - Non-comprehension<br><br>- Uses L1<br><br>- Looks to neighbour for help | Re-formulates directly to learner |
| Ingrid | 5 | - Response is quick and accurate | Uses student as a model of language pattern |

1.4a  Learner level

*AFTER THE LESSON*

1. Share and discuss your findings with the teacher of the class. Talk about any students whose level appears to be different from that designated in your meeting before the lesson.
2. During the lesson, you noted the teacher's strategies in responding appropriately to the level of the student. Some obvious accommodation strategies are listed here:

   – varying speed of language;
   – varying complexity of language;
   – varying length of wait time;
   – calling on stronger students for 'model' answers;
   – pairing and grouping arrangements.

   Can you add to this list?
3. Challenge is no doubt a good thing in the language classroom. If all students can do an activity easily and accurately then it is very probably below the appropriate level of difficulty for this class. In order to assess whether the level of difficulty is indeed appropriate, a teacher needs to be alert to the *indicators of challenge*. Some of these are listed overleaf. Can you add to this list?

*Indicators of challenge*
- Non-comprehension in facial expression
- Student wait time (= silence) before response
- First respondent does not offer the correct answer
- A learner looks sideways at a neighbour before starting writing

One investigator (Brown 1988) says that if indicators of challenge are present in about a quarter or a third of the class, then the level of challenge is about right. Would you agree?

4. What are some of the corresponding indicators of under-challenge or ease of lesson? Some of these are listed below. Can you add to the list?

*Indicators of ease*
- Student gets started quickly
- Plethora of responses to teacher's questions
- Expected time needed for tasks over-calculated

5. The question of whether to group weak students with weak and strong with strong is a vital one in teaching. There is of course no one answer that is always right. Much depends on the purpose of the group work (Austin 1990). Consider the following ways of grouping students: what outcomes might be expected in each case? Can you think of sample activities for each case?

| Ways of grouping levels | Expected outcomes | Sample activity |
|---|---|---|
| a) Group weak students together | | |
| b) Group strong students together | | |
| c) Mix the groups | | |

1.4b Grouping students according to level

6. Level is only one criterion by which groups may be created. In the chart below consider other criteria, and alongside this, indicate what the expected outcome might be, and a sample activity that would be appropriate.

| Criterion | Expected outcome | Appropiate activity |
|---|---|---|
| Own culture | 'Noisy' interaction | Discussion task – topical/social/ cultural/issue |
|  |  |  |

1.4c  Criteria for grouping students

## REFLECTION

Consider a class that you currently teach or have recently taught. How aware are you of the levels within the class? How keenly is this awareness reflected in your teaching? What aspect of your lesson most reflects this awareness? Is it possible to extend this awareness to other elements of the learning situation?

## 1.5 The learner as cultural being

### BACKGROUND

It has become axiomatic to draw attention to the inextricable bond between language and culture. Our awareness of the cultural dimension in language teaching touches a number of areas. For example, we are aware that:

— when learning a language a learner is also learning (about) a culture;
— a learner is a cultural being with a cultural perspective on the world, including culture-specific expectations of the classroom and learning processes;
— the cultural dimension of the learner has to be considered and respected;
— a positive attitude towards the culture of the target language is a favourable factor in language learning.

### TASK OBJECTIVE

The objective of this observation is to render more visible the cultural factor in the classroom and the various aspects of teaching and learning that culture permeates.

### PROCEDURE

*BEFORE THE LESSON*

1. Arrange to observe a lesson. Speak to the teacher in advance of the lesson and discuss the cultural composition of the class.
2. Make yourself familiar with the chart opposite.

*DURING THE LESSON*

1. While the lesson is in progress, observe what happens from the perspective of how culture is involved. For example, you may consider that the materials used reflect a certain pattern of native speaker behaviour; or you may consider that certain aspects of a topic have not been discussed and the reasons for this are cultural ones; you may note that the way people address and interact with each other is affected by cultural factors.
2. Some categories have been suggested in the chart opposite; add any others that are relevant. Take notes on points that are relevant to the issue of culture in language teaching.

| Categories | Notes |
| --- | --- |
| Choice of materials | |
| Choice of topics | |
| Choice of activities | |
| Teaching/learning strategies | |
| Modes of address | |
| Patterns of interaction | |
| Seating arrangements | |

## 1.5  The learner as cultural being

*AFTER THE LESSON*

1. Discuss your notes and observations from the lesson with the classroom teacher. Consider the extent to which cultural factors consciously or subconsciously affect planning and teaching.
2. To what extent should a language teacher *actively* teach the culture of the target language? Should this take the form of information about the culture or should it be at a more experiential level?
3. What ways exist for an active teaching of culture? And what ways exist for a subtle style of teaching it? Brainstorm a taxonomy of culture-teaching methodologies.
4. To what extent do you believe that 'acculturation' is a teachable concept? Do all learners of a language need to acculturate and if so, to the same extent?
5. Is the native speaker teacher of a language to be considered a cultural model of that language? If so, how are learners to differentiate among cultural, dialectal and idiolectal features of the model to which they are exposed?
6. What is the role of the non-native speaker teacher of a language in terms of the culture of that language? What special issues pertain to the teaching of culture by a non-native speaker teacher?

7. The concept of 'ego permeability' is the idea that one is more able to tune into another culture if one is less rigid about one's own. It is as if the boundaries of a person's language ego need to become flexible in order to allow the language learner to move comfortably between their own language identity and that of the target language. Ingram (1981:44) defines ego permeability as 'the extent to which [a person] can modify what he [*sic*] sees as his personal characteristics (including language characteristics) to act in a different way when operating in another culture or using another language'.

   To what extent does your experience of learning or teaching a language support this?

8. In the teaching of culture, should the emphasis be on the differences that make people cultural beings or on the universals that make people human?

9. To what extent should students of, say, English as a foreign language, be encouraged to 'be' English in the behaviour and viewpoints that underpin language? Where does this place their mother tongue and mother culture? Is there ever in this situation a potential for 'cultural imperialism' (see Rogers 1982 and Alptekin 1990)?

## REFLECTION

How do you see your role as a language teacher in relation to culture? How is this manifested in your teaching? Has your awareness of the cultural dimension been in any way altered by the experience of this observation? If so, how can you now take this awareness one step further?

# 2 Language

## 2.1 The teacher's meta-language

### BACKGROUND

The term 'meta-language' is used to mean different things. Here it is used to mean teacher talk which is not related to the language being presented: the language a teacher uses to allow the various classroom processes to happen, that is, the language of organising the classroom. This includes the teacher's explanations, response to questions, instructions, giving of praise, correction, collection of homework, etc.

While a general aim of the classroom is to minimise teacher talking time (TTT) so as to encourage student talking time (STT), meta-language itself is an important source of learning because it is genuinely communicative. For example, when a teacher praises a student or asks another one to be quiet, or sets up a task, the language used is genuinely contextualised, purposeful and communicative, and therefore a potentially rich source of input.

### TASK OBJECTIVE

This task aims to have you collect some instances of the teacher's classroom meta-language in order to consider the relative value that such language has in a learning context.

### PROCEDURE

*BEFORE THE LESSON*

1. Arrange to see a lesson, preferably with a lower-level class, and one in which the teacher plans to present 'new language'.
2. Make yourself familiar with the chart overleaf and the items you will be listening for.

## 2 Language

*DURING THE LESSON*

1. Use the chart to help you monitor the teacher's classroom language.
2. Script a chunk of teacher meta-language (do this about five times altogether during the lesson).
3. State what you understand to be the teacher's communicative purpose.
4. Briefly describe the immediate context.
5. Consider how the same meaning might be delivered to a native speaker.

| What does the teacher say? | What is the communicative purpose? | What is the immediate context? | How might this be said to a native speaker ? |
|---|---|---|---|
| 'Look at the map. Can you see the bank?' | – Giving instructions <br><br> –Checking comprehension | T. is setting up a task with a visual aid (map) | 'Can you see where the bank is (on the map) ?' |

2.1 The teacher's meta-language

*AFTER THE LESSON*

1. Consider the communicative purpose of the various teacher utterances. Consider in what ways the communication was purposeful. Was the purpose immediately obvious to the students? Consider the meta-language from the point of view of the generalisations that learners might make about the target language.

2. Look at the chunks of teacher language that you scripted. What comment would you make on the level of meta-language compared to the level of any 'formal language input' in the lesson? Is the meta-language adjusted downwards? If not, should it be? Are there any other ways open to a teacher to ease comprehension of meta-language?

3. Were any patterns evident? Willis (1981:1) writes that 'language is much better learnt through real use than through patterns and drills'. Sometimes, though, the teacher's meta-language may be seen as patterned behaviour, which may serve, over time, as a type of authentic, communicative drill.

   Were there any chunks of teacher talk that you observed that potentially might become 'pattern drills'?

4. What features of the immediate context supported the teacher's meta-language? What can a teacher do to heighten contextual clues?

5. a) The potential of meta-language to be a rich source of learning for the student raises some important issues. Widdowson (1990: 67) writes:

   > It has been traditionally supposed that the language presented to learners should be simplified in some way for easy access and acquisition. Nowadays there are recommendations that the language presented should be authentic. How is it to be graded so that it can be made accessible? Is simplification as a pedagogic strategy inconsistent with the principles of a communicative approach to language teaching?

   Here Widdowson is talking about the language actually presented as model language. However, we can apply his remarks to meta-language as well. If we believe that meta-language is a rich source of language data and potential learning to learners, then of what significance are the accommodations we make to simplify the incoming message to the learner? Do they, through simplification, help the learner access the target language or do they delay mastery by being an inauthentic model?

   b) Reflect on the notes you made in the far right column of the chart and consider whether any accommodation was made to the learner in regard to level and what sort of accommodation this was.

   c) Can we reconcile the need for meta-language to be 'easy' with the importance of learners' being surrounded by and exposed to authentic language data?

6. In groups of four, try this role-play exercise.

   A = the teacher   B = low-level student   C = native speaker
   D = observer

- A gives B instructions for doing a particular activity, for example, lighting a fire, putting on nail polish, starting a car, loading a dishwasher.
- Then A tells C the same instructions.
- D observes, takes notes, and leads the discussion at the end on the differences in language (verbal and non-verbal) between the first set of instructions and the second.

## REFLECTION

Has this task increased your awareness of issues related to classroom teacher talk? Is there anything you would like to pursue further?

## ACKNOWLEDGEMENT

The material in this task is derived in part from work by Ray Litster.

## 2.2 The language of questions

### BACKGROUND

Language teachers ask a lot of questions. Sinclair and Coulthard (1975) found that questions are one of the commonest types of utterances in the discourse of classrooms. Questions can have different purposes, for example, socialising, scene setting, checking vocabulary, checking learning and seeking opinion. While teachers often plan their questions in terms of the lesson's content, they seem to place less emphasis on considering their questions in terms of the cognitive and linguistic demands made on the learner. These demands relate to both decoding the question and encoding the response.

### TASK OBJECTIVE

This task aims to have you collect some questions and question-and-answer sets from a language lesson. The data collected will be classified and analysed.

### PROCEDURE

*BEFORE THE LESSON*

1. Arrange to observe a lesson.
2. Read right through this task.

*DURING THE LESSON*

1. Listen carefully to the teacher's questions. Collect about twenty of these in roughly chronological order.
2. Now listen for some teacher question–student answer 'sets'. A set here means an exchange between teacher and student, initiated by the teacher's question. It might be as simple as a pair: for example, teacher question + student answer; or more complex: for example, teacher question + teacher reformulation + student response + another student response. The boundaries of the set are usually quite clear.

    Try to record about five of these faithfully. They may come from anywhere in the lesson.

*AFTER THE LESSON*

1. Looking first at the twenty single questions you have collected, consider these from the point of view of the expected response. It may help to write in a sample response for each question.
2. Now classify the questions into categories on the basis of the expected response. Some suggested categories are given below. There is some overlap among these, and of course other categories might be used instead of or in addition to these. You may like to set up a number of binary categories and classify questions accordingly, for example, questions that require students to share previous knowledge versus those that require information just presented; or questions for which the teacher is seeking a 'form' answer versus questions where the teacher is interested in the meaning of the response.

    Here are some other question types. It may help to decide first on the framework you will be working with.

    - *Yes/no questions*, e.g. 'Here is a picture of a woman. Have you seen her face before?'
    - *Short answer/retrieval-style questions*, e.g. 'What did she say about the film?'
    - *Open-ended questions*, e.g. 'Whom could he have telephoned?'
    - *Display questions* (questions requesting information already known to the questioner), e.g. 'What colour is this pen?'
    - *Referential questions* (questions requesting new information), e.g. 'What did you study at university?'
    - *Non-retrieval, imaginative questions* (questions that do not require the learner to retrieve given information but instead call on inferred information or information in which an opinion or judgement is called for), e.g. 'What do you think the writer was suggesting by making the central character an animal?'

3. What *pattern*, if any, emerges from the classification of your questions? Can you point to any *factors* that might help account for this, for example, the type of lesson it was, the stage of the lesson from which the questions came, the age of the students, etc.?
4. Consider the notion of *difficulty* from the learner's point of view. Rank a selection of your collected questions on to a cline of easy → more difficult → difficult. What are the factors that increase difficulty?
5. Consider now the *question-and-answer sets* you have recorded. Rank the five in order of complexity of response so that (1) will be the response requiring the least challenge to the student and (5) will be the response requiring the greatest challenge.
6. Is there any correlation between the *type of question* and the *complexity of response* elicited?
7. What comment can you make on this remark:

> The teacher must have a clear and explicit understanding of the nature of the challenge to students' internal representation of knowledge that a particular question may present . . . They must appreciate the level of cognitive difficulty involved in the students' effort to respond to a particular question. (Tollefson 1989)

## REFLECTION

Using this observation as a mirror of your own teaching, consider how you approach the design of questions in your lessons. Has this observation in any way increased your awareness of the skill of questioning? If you were to pursue this line of thinking in relation to your teaching, what aspects would you be keen to explore?

## 2.3 The language of feedback to error

### BACKGROUND

The language of feedback refers to the responses given by the teacher to what learners produce in the classroom. In its most narrow definition, this refers to teacher response to error. Most teachers are aware of feedback in terms of its motivational value – the value of positive feedback and the dis-incentive that negative reinforcement can produce. However, apart from the motivational aspects of providing feedback, there are linguistic and cognitive reasons for teachers to consider closely how they respond. The exact content of the teacher's response as it relates to the learner's production may well have an important influence on the learning process.

### TASK OBJECTIVE

You will be observing a lesson in order to concentrate on the language of feedback to error. This means recording/collecting data of a number of student–teacher interactions, often with four *utterance components*: teacher question + student response + teacher feedback + student response to feedback.

### PROCEDURE

*BEFORE THE LESSON*

1. Arrange to observe a lesson.
2. Make yourself familiar with the four-utterance paradigm that you are seeking (see example overleaf).

*DURING THE LESSON*

1. Collect some samples of the four-utterance paradigm. We are especially looking for examples that include learner error and teacher feedback to error. It does not matter if they do not all fit neatly into the sample schema.
2. Wherever you can, note any non-verbal and supplementary support that is given to the information, for example, use of the board, visual, gesture.
3. Consider whether the feedback was generally positive and encouraging (+) or negative and discouraging (−).

| Sample | Supplementary support | + / − |
|---|---|---|
| Teacher question | | |
| Student response | | |
| Teacher feedback | | |
| Student response to feedback | | |

## 2.3 The language of feedback to error

*AFTER THE LESSON*

1. Feedback, according to Brown (1988:16), has to be genuinely responsive: 'It means allowing learners to experience the effect of what they produce as a guide . . . in their future efforts.' Brown believes that feedback must be more than encouragement, for 'empty and automatic encouragement is often pointless' (*ibid.*). A genuine response from the teacher provides some indication to learners of the effectiveness of their utterances.

   What implications do you think this has for the language of teacher feedback? Consider the data collected during this lesson in the light of whether the learners 'experienced the effect' of their errors through their teacher.

2. It has been said (Zamel 1981) that the information component of teacher feedback is crucial to the learner's learning process. According to Zamel, feedback is most effective when it:

   − points out critical features of the language;
   − gives information that allows the student 'to discover by oneself' rules and principles of language;
   − reduces ambiguity of choice for the learner.

   Analyse the data you have collected. Look closely at the *information content* of the teacher's feedback. To what extent is the teacher, in the feedback, providing for the learner:

- information that explicitly and specifically highlights where the error is?
- information that defines what the choices are, thereby reducing the alternatives open to the learner?
- information that helps the learner correctly adjust their current understanding?

3. On the basis of your analysis, comment now on the language of feedback in these terms:

   a) Was the information supported by other messages through different media, such as gesture, visual?
   b) Was the message appropriately limited (not overloaded)? Did it reduce, rather than increase, ambiguity?

4. The assumption underlying the considerations given here to the language of feedback is that the language learner is 'an active and selective information-gatherer who acquires and interprets new information on the basis of rules already stored in the brain' (Smith 1971).

   This is a cognitive rather than a behaviourist view of the learner: students have their own 'criterial sets', their own understanding of how the language is organised. Each production of language is a testing out of internal hypotheses. Feedback from the teacher may result in a slight adjustment of the original hypotheses.

   To what extent do you agree or disagree with this view of the language learner and language learning? Why may it cause confusion to say 'good' to a wrong answer?

5. Do you agree with the view that one of the teacher's key roles in the classroom is to provide accurate feedback on error to learners?

6. With regard to classroom roles, consider this statement:

   The teacher's output becomes the input for the student and determines future performance and the student's output becomes the input for the teacher and determines the reaction to that performance . . . Teaching and learning are no longer exclusive roles; they become the provinces of both performers in the classroom: while the teacher instructs, the teacher learns about what must be done next, and while the learner learns, the student gives instruction about what information is lacking.

   (Zamel 1981: 149)

7. When you collected the data for this task you also noted whether the teacher's response was encouraging or discouraging from the perspective of the learner. To what extent do you consider that the teacher's role, in response to feedback, has a motivational function? Some teachers, for example, consider that they should not be involved in praise or criticism of the students (Edge 1989). Some claim this is the case with adult learners but that children require

more overt teacher approval/disapproval in their learning processes. Where do you stand in your views?

## REFLECTION

Using the experience of observing and analysing the language of feedback as a mirror of your own teaching, what insights have emerged? How might you discover more about your own language of feedback?

## 2.4 Language echoes

### BACKGROUND

A distinctive feature of the classroom, and perhaps more especially the language learning classroom, are 'echoes' – the teacher utterances which echo students' responses but produce no response themselves. In terms of classroom discourse, they do not further an exchange; they are in fact 'dead ends'.

Perhaps the best way to illustrate this concept is through example. Of the following examples (Lindstromberg 1988) only (a) is an echo, as here the teacher's returning utterance provides no response to the student. In both (b) and (c) the teacher has processed the student's language and this is indicated in the response.

a) T: And what do you think?
   S: He's coming later.
   T: (no change of intonation) He's coming later.

b) S: He's coming lately.
   T: He's coming . . .? (teacher elicits response)
   S: Lately?
   T: Later. (teacher substitutes correction)

c) T: And what do you think?
   S: He's coming later.
   T: He's coming later? (teacher asks *yes/no* question for confirmation)
   S: Yes.

## TASK OBJECTIVE

The aim of this task is to raise awareness of the issue of teacher echoes in classroom discourse. You will collect a number of teacher–student exchanges. This will lead to an analysis of the data and a consideration of the pros and cons of this aspect of teacher behaviour.

## PROCEDURE

*BEFORE THE LESSON*

1. Arrange to observe a lesson.
2. Make yourself familiar with the way 'echoing' is defined (see examples above).

*DURING THE LESSON*

1. Spend some time (five to ten minutes) becoming 'attuned' to the way the teacher responds to the learners, listening for echoes.
2. Then try to script about three samples of teacher echoes. Include the immediate 'environment', and, typically two or three utterances leading up to the teacher echo.
3. Then select a portion of time (say fifteen minutes), preferably during a time of the lesson involving teacher–student interaction, and count the number of echoes that occur in this time.

*AFTER THE LESSON*

1. How many 'echoes' did you collect? To what extent do you think the teacher's behaviour was conscious or subconscious?
2. What is the effect of the teacher's echo on:

   a) the learner, immediately?
   b) patterns of classroom interaction generally?
   c) on the learner's perception of the teacher's corrective role?
   d) on the learner's willingness to take risks?

3. Considering the three samples you collected, would you agree that teacher echoes are 'dead ends'?
4. What kind of information do learners need in feedback received from teachers? Using these terms of reference, how does 'the echo' rate as valid or valuable feedback?
5. Some points in favour of echoing (see Lindstromberg 1988) have been the following:

   – it provides learners with the repetition needed for reinforcement of language;

- it gets over the problem of contributions from students who speak very quietly;
- it gets over the problem of poor pronunciation by providing intelligible versions for the whole class;
- it can be used as a strategy to provide models of correctness in the event of error.

How do you respond to each of these?

6. One common criticism of echoing is that an echo is 'not a natural response': that is, it is unlikely to occur in contexts outside of the classroom (although it might appear in some forms of therapy).

   a) Is it true that echoing is an almost exclusively classroom-based discourse feature? How is it different from the sort of repetition that occurs very naturally in conversation routines?

   b) Does a discourse feature have to have a 'reality' outside of the classroom in order for it to be 'acceptable' inside it?

## REFLECTION

How can you find out whether or not echoing features significantly in your own teaching discourse? Are you interested in monitoring this aspect of teacher behaviour?

## 2.5  Language as the negotiation of meaning

### BACKGROUND

During the last decade of language learning research, interlanguage studies (e.g. Doughty and Pica 1986; Long and Porter 1985) have revealed that the language used by learners in the classroom, in the actual processes of engaging with materials and with each other, is a significant factor in their language learning. ('Interlanguage' refers to the language produced by non-native speaking learners who are in the process of learning.)

The term *conversational modification*, used by Doughty and Pica (1986), refers to the various means by which learners negotiate the meaning of input so as to make it comprehensible and personally meaningful. The inference is that when learners are compelled to negotiate their own meaning, the very process of so doing is an aid to their language learning. Conversational modification takes place via a number of key procedures which are detailed on the following page.

## TASK OBJECTIVE

The objective of this task is to sensitise you to the language of conversational modification and to the factors that promote it.

## PROCEDURE

*BEFORE THE LESSON*

1. Arrange to observe a lesson in which you might expect there to be a good deal of conversational modification. Research findings suggest that certain lesson types are more conducive than others to the generation of conversational modification, for example, lessons in which there is:

   - an obvious degree of challenge built into the lesson;
   - a focus on meaning rather than correct form:
   - a task in which learners engage in an information-gap exercise where the members of the group rely on each other's information in order to complete the task.

2. Make yourself familiar with the following categories of language operations through which meaning may be negotiated (Doughty and Pica 1986: 313).

*A confirmation check*

This is where the listener believes they have understood but wishes to make certain, for example:

A: Mexican food have a lot of ulcers.
B: Mexicans have a lot of ulcers? Because of the food?

*A comprehension check*

This is where the speaker wants to make certain that the listener has understood, for example:

A: Do you know what I mean?

*A clarification request*

This is when one interlocutor does not entirely comprehend the meaning and asks for clarification, for example:

A: She's on welfare.
B: What do you mean by welfare?

*A repetition*

This is where the speaker repeats (or re-states) their own (or another's utterance) in order to repair a real (or perceived) communication breakdown, for example:

A: She's on welfare.
B: I think she's working at the factory.
C: No, she lost her job. She's on welfare.

DURING THE LESSON

Through a portion of the lesson, use the chart below and try to record some instances of language operations used by learners, in contact with each other or with the teacher, that modify conversation in such a way as to negotiate meaning. This may involve your sitting with a group during a task activity or using a tape recorder.

In each case try to record in the *Language* column the initial utterance, the response and the return (if any). Also indicate the participants involved. Later you will consider what type of operation it was and whether it was successful in negotiating meaning.

| Language | Participants | Type of operation | Success of outcome |
|---|---|---|---|
| A: | A= | | |
| B: | B= | | |
| A: | | | |

2.5 Language as the negotiation of meaning

AFTER THE LESSON

1. Consider the two right-hand columns of your chart. Try to classify the data collected according to what type of language operation was used. In each case, too, comment on the outcome: was the negotiation of meaning successful?

2. What sort of factors are conducive to creating a learning context in which conversational modification happens? Some of these have been mentioned earlier (see *Before the lesson*).
3. Do you think that learning that requires students to undergo some of the typical processes of meaning negotiation is an asset to the learning, or an unnecessary challenge for learners?
4. According to Brown (1988: 9) teachers should aim towards developing the skill that 'encourage[s] learners to resort to conversational modification when necessary to make meanings clear'. This has a strong implication for a teacher's 'indulgence' towards error. What do you consider is the link between teacher tolerance of error and learner negotiation of meaning?
5. The type of teaching that encourages conversational modification is very different from the type of teaching where error is minimised. What do you think are the assumptions behind language learning and teaching in these kinds of teaching?

## REFLECTION

Reflecting on your own teaching, what will you take back into your own teaching from this observation?

# 3 Learning

## 3.1 The learning environment

### BACKGROUND

Few would now doubt that people learn best when they are relaxed, comfortable, unstressed, interested and involved in what is going on, and motivated to continue. Regrettably, there is no hard-and-fast, definitive list of what makes an environment conducive to learning. We cannot, for example, say that 'the more a teacher smiles, the more relaxed the students are' as this is absurdly simplistic. Nonetheless, there may be a lot to be gained from developing an awareness of the affective factors that influence learning.

### TASK OBJECTIVE

This observation is designed to refine your awareness of the learning environment. During the lesson you will be watching and listening for anything that you think contributes to making the learning environment one in which students learn better. Conversely, you will also become aware of factors that hinder or impede learning and detract from the effectiveness of the learning environment.

Broadly, then, you are looking for factors that range from the size of the room, the seating arrangements, the acoustics, aspects of the teacher's behaviour or the classroom dynamics. You will also, for a short period during the lesson, focus on one student and note the external factors during that period that seem to shape their learning involvement.

One difficulty in this task is that the very presence of 'an outsider' among the learning community will affect it in subtle, perhaps imperceptible ways. This is difficult to avoid but might be minimised by your awareness and your maintaining a very low profile.

## PROCEDURE

*BEFORE THE LESSON*

1. Arrange to observe a lesson. Try to avoid lessons with a heavy emphasis on reading and writing as there may not be very much to observe in Step 4 below.
2. Make yourself familiar with the charts overleaf.

*DURING THE LESSON*

1. Seat yourself in a place where you have a clear view of the classroom, and yet where your presence will be as unobtrusive as possible.
2. For most of the lesson, concentrate on making yourself as aware as possible of the affective environment, the ambience in the classroom, and the various and diverse factors that are influential here. Consider factors that are external to the student, such as the acoustics or temperature of the room, the comfort or otherwise of the seating, the visual attraction of the room, the quality, tone or volume of the teacher's voice.
3. Record these (see Chart 3.1a) in any order, as you become aware of them. (A follow-up task after the lesson will be to analyse the data and group items into categories. For the moment a 'raw' list is adequate.)
   List these under *Factor/item*. The column *Memory jog* allows you space for a brief note (for example, phase of lesson, context) to record information to help you remember the detail.
4. The second task requires you to graph one student's concentration in the lesson. It is important to be aware that both internal and external factors are relevant here, but that because internal factors are unobservable, we will be gauging concentration through external evidence alone. In addition, you may like to use face drawings (see Chart 3.1b) to indicate mood (Woodward 1991).
   Take about twelve minutes out of the above activity to concentrate on one student in the class. Choose someone you have a good view of but try not to make them aware of your attentions. Use Chart 3.1b to help you. The horizontal axis records the degree of concentration. At each point marked on the vertical axis, note what was happening to or around the student, for example: T's question, S doodling on paper, S gazing around room, S copying notes from board.

| Factor/item | Memory jog |
|---|---|
| - *Large room, well ventilated*<br><br>- *Positive T response to SS -*<br>  *encouraging* | -<br><br>- *Elicitation phase*<br>  *7 mins into*<br>  *lesson* |

3.1a  Affective factors in the learning environment

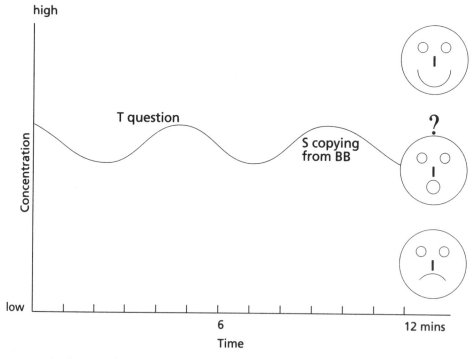

3.1b  Graph of a student's concentration pattern over 12 minutes

*AFTER THE LESSON*

1. Consider the information you have included in the column *Factor/item*. Look at chart 3.1c and try to group factors into categories, for example: physical factors (room size, ventilation); teaching behaviour (style of positive reinforcement, e.g. smile, nod).

| A | B | C | D |
|---|---|---|---|
| Physical factors | Teacher behaviour | | |
| Room size<br><br>Ventilation | Smiles<br><br>Nods<br><br>Calls by name | | |

3.1c Categories

2. Comment on anything you observed that:
   - surprised you;
   - puzzled you;
   - concerned you;
   - inspired you.

3. Reflecting on the overall ambience in the classroom, what general patterns or tendencies emerged? Are these related to any language patterns noticeable in the classroom? Would you venture any generalisations based on what you have uncovered here? Consider, too, the extent to which we are entitled to generalise about something internal and invisible (that is, learning) from external signs or symptoms.

4. Consider now Chart 3.1b, where you graphed one student's concentration, and possibly mood(s), over a portion of the lesson. Comment on the external factors that seemed to affect or shape the student's concentration.

5. Teacher trainers are often at pains to emphasise that there is no such thing as one good or ideal teaching style, that there are as many styles as there are teachers.

   a) Do you agree?
   b) Are there stylistic features that one associates with good language teaching?
   c) How 'teachable' and 'learnable' is the concept of style?

## REFLECTION

If you were asked to describe the sort of learning environment characteristic of the classrooms where you teach, what would you say? Can you identify any conscious strategies you use to generate this environment?

## 3.2   Checking learning

### BACKGROUND

If all students learned what they were taught at the time at which it was
first taught, and if all of them grasped it equally well and equally
quickly, teaching would be much less complex than it is. In fact, of
course, learners do not always learn what the teacher sets out to teach –
sometimes they learn less, and sometimes other (more valuable?) things!
Nor do they all learn in the same way or at the same rate. In fact, little
about the elements is predictable or generalisable across a class of
learners. It is for this reason that teachers develop strategies for checking
that learning is taking place or has taken place.

### TASK OBJECTIVE

This observation task is designed to help you monitor learning by
monitoring a teacher's monitoring of learning. You will be looking at
the language used in monitoring learning and analysing what each
learning check achieves.

### PROCEDURE

*BEFORE THE LESSON*

1. Arrange to observe a lesson, preferably one that will involve the
   presentation of new language.
2. Pay attention to the stated objective of the lesson.
3. Make yourself familiar with the chart opposite and the particular
   items you will be attending to.

*DURING THE LESSON*

Use the chart to help you monitor how the teacher monitors learners'
understanding. Collect about five instances of teacher checking.

1. Script the teacher's language (including any non-verbal signals) used
   to check learning.
2. In each case, what is the teacher checking?
3. Can you identify the trigger that prompted the teacher to check, for
   example, a student appearing confused; a necessary logical step in the
   lesson; repeated and similar errors by a number of students?
4. How does the student respond to the check?
5. What, if any, follow-up happens?
6. What did the learning check achieve?

7. Try also to be aware of times in the lesson when the teacher did not check for learning, but you would have; or where the teacher did, but you would not have.

| 1 | 2 | 3 | 4 | 5 | 6 |
|---|---|---|---|---|---|
| *How does teacher check?* | *What does teacher check?* | *Why does teacher check?* | *How does student respond?* | *What follow-up is there?* | *What did the learning check achieve?* |
| 'Is she still fat?' | Time focus in 'used to'? | To establish concept of new language | 'No, she isn't.' | T confirms ('That's right'), checks another S | Establishes + confirms meaning, leads on to next phase of lesson |

3.2 Checking learning

*AFTER THE LESSON*

1. Share the collected data with the teacher and discuss the checking process as seen from the teacher's point of view.
2. Reflect on the last column – what did the learning check achieve? Add any relevant information to your grid.
3. Looking over the five instances of checking that you collected, is it possible to do any of the following:

   – label them?
   – group them according to any similarities?
   – rank them, indicating your criterion?

   Is it possible to say that questions that check for learning tend to be of a particular type? If you agree, try to describe in greater detail the type of question we are referring to here.
4. Generally, was there a neat link between the purpose for the check (Column 3) and the results of the check (Column 6)? If not, what factors are relevant here?

5. Were there times in the lesson when *you* would have checked learning but where the teacher did not? (Or where you would not have, but the teacher did?) Think about *what* and *why* you would have checked and how that varied from what happened in the lesson. Perhaps discuss these points with the teacher.

6. Consider again the stated objective of the lesson you observed. Was it achieved? How do you know? Did the learning checks in any way seem to propel the lesson onwards towards its objective? Did the monitoring of learning in the lesson have any connection with the reaching of or failure to reach the lesson's objective?

7. Learning involves processing information and appraising new information in the light of previous understanding. What evidence did you notice through the lesson of the learners' processing meaning, for example, the meaning of new concepts, structures, vocabulary? To what extent, in the lesson you observed, did the monitoring of learning allow the teacher 'to tap into the student's head' and guess at the state of the processing of meaning?

8. Have you any comment to make on how monitoring of learning might influence the sorts of decisions that a teacher makes in the classroom?

## REFLECTION

In regard to how this observation has raised your awareness, comment on the experience by deciding which of the following applies:

— in this lesson I found what I already knew, and have now confirmed it;
— in this lesson I found what I suspected but had never thoughtfully considered;
— in this lesson I found what I had not considered before;
— in this lesson I found what I would like to pursue further.

## 3.3　Learning and teaching compared

### BACKGROUND

It has long been known that teaching does not equal learning – that what a teacher goes into a classroom to teach may not match what the learner perceives the lesson to be about or what learning is achieved on the part of the learner. This is because the construction of meaning is an essentially personal experience for each individual.

This unit is concerned with how, as Allwright claims (1988), 'each lesson is a different lesson for every learner'. We will be examining how a teaching plan appears to be realised in learning terms in the minds of learners.

The difficulty in this type of task, as in many aspects of observing learning, is that learning itself is not directly visible. Teaching aims, for example, should not be confused with learning outcomes, as these will vary according, in part, to how the learner acts on the input. We therefore must guard against making simplistic equations or drawing conclusions about learning based only on observable data. With these reservations in mind, we might proceed to consider how learning appears to be happening for some learners.

### TASK OBJECTIVE

In this task you will collaborate with another observer to compare the learning contributions made by different learners in order to see how the same teaching seems to translate for different learners.

### PROCEDURE

This task can be conducted in one of two ways:

a) You may tape-record the interaction of one pair working on a task set as part of a lesson. The transcribed interaction then becomes the subject of scrutiny.
b) You may observe a lesson, along with a colleague, and each of you will concentrate on a different learner within the same group, and later compare your notes.

If you choose to conduct a live observation, follow the instructions for *During the lesson* overleaf. If on the other hand you use a transcription, apply the same instructions to the transcription.

# 3 Learning

1. Arrange to observe or tape-record a lesson.
2. Make yourself familiar with the lesson plan, the teaching aims, and with the procedure outlined below.

*DURING THE LESSON*

During the paired task, each observer should focus on one of the pair (X or Y). Take notes on the interaction, following these guidelines:

a) What does X (or Y) do?
b) What does X (or Y) seem to want to learn?
c) What, in your opinion, might X (or Y) have learned from this lesson?

*AFTER THE LESSON*

1. Compare your respective analyses of X and Y. Use these questions to guide you:

    a) How do they compare?
    b) How different was this experience for each of them?
    c) What difference does each make to the experience of the other?
    d) What difference does the teacher make?
    e) To what extent is your analysis compromised by the subjectivity of the observation process?

2. Learning involves a processing – via construction and reconstruction – of meaning that is personally significant and relevant to the learner (Williams 1989). Re-appraising old information to bring it in line with new is what constitutes learning.

    What evidence did you find of this type of processing in your observation and analysis of the students in this lesson?

3. Allwright believes that teacher-created lesson plans, whether they be rigid or flexible, tend to overlook the 'reality' of what students bring to the classroom.

    What are some of the things that students bring to the classroom that will affect the course of their learning?

4. If each lesson is a different lesson for every learner, how can a teacher plan to accommodate and cater for a class of students?

5. What are the implications for the mismatch between teaching/learning for:

    – teacher preparation of lessons?
    – teacher decision-making in the classroom?
    – curriculum planning?

6. If you were able to ask the students at the end of the lesson what they thought they had learned, what do you think some of the responses

might be? To what extent does this align with the stated objectives of the lesson?

In regard to this, you may like to observe another lesson and, with the teacher's permission, follow it up with a survey of individual students to see what they think the lesson was aiming to do.

## REFLECTION

You might like to apply the experience of this observation to your own teaching. At the end of a lesson, ask the students to consider what they thought the intended aim of the lesson was. Then compare it with your intended aim. This may throw some light on the match-up between teaching and learning.

## ACKNOWLEDGEMENT

This task was largely derived from the experience of attending Dick Allwright's seminar on this topic at the 6th ATESOL Summer School in Sydney, Australia, in January 1988.

## 3.4 Learning aims

### BACKGROUND

A key factor in the planning and organisation of learning is an understanding of aims. One way of clarifying and classifying aims is that offered by Brown (1988) who differentiates between pedagogic, language learning and social aims:

1. *Pedagogic aims*: these are the overall syllabus goals, both short- and long-term.
2. *Language learning aims*: this is at the lesson level and relates to why learners are asked to do what they do at any phase or sub-phase of a lesson.
3. *Social aims*: these relate to the social climate in the classroom and the sorts of roles that will be expected of learners.

Another way of perceiving and classifying aims is at the two levels of task and language (M. Williams, personal correspondence). At the task level, the aims are often non-linguistic, for example, finding out about other class members' attitudes to a topic through questions based on a survey. At the level of language, the task is underpinned by linguistic aims, for example, practising the language of information-seeking based on a survey of attitudes.

As with observing many aspects of learning, we have to bear in mind that a large part of what is cogent to our understanding happens invisibly, that is, is internal to the learner. Another related danger is that of setting up a one-to-one correspondence between teaching aims and learning outcomes. We need, despite the great difficulty involved, to consider the way the learner acts on the input provided through a lesson. Awareness of these points will prevent our understanding from being limited to purely observable data.

## TASK OBJECTIVE

This task is designed to increase awareness of learning aims and how these relate to the actual lesson taught. One question to be considered is the extent to which the aims, as perceived and planned by the teacher, are shared with or made available to the learner. After the lesson we will consider whether learners benefit from being aware of the lesson's aims and how these fit into the overall scheme.

## PROCEDURE

*BEFORE THE LESSON*

1. Arrange to observe a lesson. Meet with the teacher in advance and discuss the lesson's aims.
2. Make a list of these aims using the chart opposite.

*DURING THE LESSON*

1. As you observe the lesson, note in the middle column whether (and if so, how) the teacher's aims were made explicit to the learners.
2. In the right-hand column include any field notes to show how learners became aware of the aims of the lesson through the teacher's language or actions.

| Teacher's aims | Were aims made explicit? How? | Field notes |
|---|---|---|
| | | *'Today we are going to...'* |

### 3.4a Learning aims

*AFTER THE LESSON*

1. Discuss the lesson with the teacher, sharing your notes as a basis for discussion. To what extent do your impressions concur with the teacher's intentions? Consider, too, the extent to which the learners were 'inducted' into the lesson's aims.

2. Consider once again the list of teaching aims that you noted down before the lesson. This may have been noted down in random order. This time, re-consider the aims and note them down in schematic form, either grouping them in a particular way, or ranking them on a scale of importance or on a scale using a different criterion. To what extent did the reality of the lesson fulfil the teaching aims? It could be valuable to discuss these issues with the teacher too and compare impressions.

3. Do learners need to know what the lesson aims to do? One opinion is that this is level-dependent – for example, some upper-level learners have a clear idea of their own learning purposes, goals and pathways, and expect to be 'knowing participants' in the determining of learning aims.

    Is it always the case that learners ought to be aware of where the teacher is heading and how they intend getting there? Would you qualify this assertion in any way? Consider the relevant factors that would determine how much you would include learners as knowing participants.

4. Consider two extremes of classroom types. In Classroom A, the teacher's aims are something written on the lesson plan or kept in the

teacher's head but not shared with the students. In Classroom B, the lesson might begin with the teacher explaining how this lesson fits into the weekly programme. The teacher then states what the aims of the lesson are and at key phases through the lesson explains the reason behind what the students are being asked to do.

Using the chart below, reflect on what the two different styles reveal of the teachers' theories of:

— how people learn;
— the roles of teacher and learners;
— who holds responsibility for learning;

and any other underlying premises you consider relevant.

| Premises | Classroom A | Classroom B |
|---|---|---|
| How people learn | | |
| Teacher/learner roles | | |
| Responsibility for learning | | |

3.4b  Teachers' underlying theories

5.  Comment on the linkage between what a teacher sets out to achieve and the tools and processes of evaluation.

**REFLECTION**

To what extent do you plan out aims for your teaching? Do you group these aims in any meaningful way? To what extent are learners aware of the aims you hold for them when you teach? Reflect on the premises that underpin your decision-making in these regards.

## 3.5  Lexis and learning

**BACKGROUND**

Traditionally, lexis has not been given pride of place in teachers' priorities, serving more as a cushion on which to practise grammar patterns than as an important section of the learning curriculum in its own right. This contrasts strikingly with learners' perceptions about vocabulary: very often learners equate language learning with learning new labels for familiar concepts. Recent research (e.g. Lipa 1990) shows too a difference between teacher and learner perceptions of vocabulary difficulty.

**TASK OBJECTIVE**

This task concentrates on the place of lexis in language teaching and learning. Specifically, it contrasts teachers' and learners' perceptions of vocabulary difficulty.

**PROCEDURE**

*BEFORE THE LESSON*

1.  Arrange to observe a lesson, preferably one that incorporates a text, aural or written.
2.  Before the lesson, meet with the teacher and discuss the vocabulary of the text. Find out from the teacher which words they consider will be difficult for the learners and note them in the chart overleaf. ('Difficult' here means words the students cannot understand, and which are felt to impede comprehension of the text.) Tell the teacher you want to ask the students to write a list of what they think are difficult words (see Step 2).
3.  Also by way of preparation, analyse the text and note down which words *you* perceive will be difficult for the students. Use the chart to help you record your perceptions of difficulty.

*DURING THE LESSON*

1.  Monitor students' perceptions of the text, in particular which words they find difficult. Complete the chart accordingly.
2.  At the end of the lesson, with the teacher's permission, take ten minutes to ask students to write down a list of what they consider to be the difficult words. This will give you a wider sampling than mere classroom monitoring.

| Words perceived to be difficult: | | |
|---|---|---|
| by the teacher | by you | by the learners |
| | | |

3.5 Lexis and learning

*AFTER THE LESSON*

1. Collate the students' lists so that you can better compare/contrast their perceptions with yours and the teacher's. To what extent do they overlap?
2. In experiments conducted on perceptions of difficulty in vocabulary, where there was quite a variance between teachers' and students' perceptions (Lipa 1990: 157–66) one of the implications given was that teaching should proceed on the understanding that there is a potential for a difference of perceptions: 'we should invite our students to indicate what they find difficult in . . . a passage, and having listed their contributions according to frequency of choice, allow them to deal co-operatively with explanations of meaning.'
   What is your view here?
3. Research conducted by Willing (1988) suggests that students give a very high weighting to the value of vocabulary in language learning, much higher than teachers' weighting. One implication of this is that we perhaps should be directly asking our students *how they learn vocabulary and how they want to be taught*, and we should then heed in our teaching the students' statements on learning preferences.
   What is your view?
4. Teachers use a range of strategies to help clarify the meaning of difficult words. Consider the arguments for:

- pre-teaching (fill in the hole before you get to it) versus teaching difficult words in text (fall in the hole when you get to it);
- word lists versus teaching individual words in context;
- target-language-only versus translated equivalents.

## REFLECTION

What does this experience mirror of your own foreign language learning? What does it mirror of your own teaching? What aspects of your own teaching of vocabulary have you been stimulated to consider or re-appraise?

# 4 The lesson

## 4.1 Lesson planning

### BACKGROUND

Very often, lesson planning begins with a sheet of paper and an objective or set of objectives, and works its way through a number of procedures, steps and phases through to the end.

In this observation we will be approaching lesson design from a different departure point – from the perspective of the completed lesson. We will be working backwards from a taught lesson to determine what decisions were made by the teacher in planning this lesson. The planning of teaching is seen as a series of decisions made by a teacher about the various elements of a lesson – learners, materials, tasks, etc.

A key point to be stressed is that while planning is a relatively static activity, teaching is inherently dynamic. It follows therefore that, in a sense, plans are made to be changed – that is, they are drawn up in the knowledge that the teacher will almost inevitably alter the plan as the lesson develops. These 'up-and-running' decisions are no less important than those made before the lesson began.

### TASK OBJECTIVE

The task objective is to determine – through a set of a focussed and guided questions – what decisions the teacher made in planning the lesson. As we shall see, the planning refers both to preparation before the lesson and decisions taken in the classroom during the lesson. Changes to plans and reasons for them will be an important element in the post-lesson consultation with the teacher.

### PROCEDURE

*BEFORE THE LESSON*

Arrange to observe a lesson. It does not matter what sort of lesson it is, as long as it is one which involves the teacher in some thought, planning or preparation. It may help to have a copy of the lesson plan while observing the lesson in order to distinguish between pre-planned and on-the-spot teacher decisions. After the lesson you will be discussing the planning elements with the teacher.

*DURING THE LESSON*

1. Below is a list of questions about various aspects of planning language teaching. Of course the nature of the lesson will determine the relevance of these: a lesson devoted to role-play will be different from a writing lesson or one devoted to an analysis of grammar. Choose, therefore, the aspects that are relevant to the lesson you observe.

---

In observing this lesson, what inferences can you make concerning the teacher's decisions about:

1 establishing a certain classroom atmosphere?
2 motivating the students to the lesson?
3 realistically contextualising language?
4 involving the students and drawing out passive knowledge?
5 lexis: how much to teach? What? When? And how?
6 checking for comprehension and learning?
7 providing safe contexts for practice?
8 helping students to identify rules and organise new knowledge?
9 shifting the focus and patterns of interaction?
10 setting up activities that promote communication?
11 establishing a framework in which students work without the teacher?
12 the aids to be used in various parts of the lesson?
13 integrating skills involved in the lesson?
14 how information is to be organised and shared?
15 ending the lesson and linking it to previous/future ones?

---

## 4 The lesson

This chart will help with recording data:

| Observation | Inference | Discussion questions |
|---|---|---|
| *T uses pictures and realia to explain meaning of words* | *Evidence of planning - these words considered potentially difficult* | *How were the difficult words chosen?* |

4.1 Lesson planning

2. As the lesson develops there may be questions that you yourself would like to ask the teacher about the various decisions taken about the lesson. Make a note of these as they emerge during the lesson.

   At the end of the lesson your notes will offer a reconstitution of the original plan plus the changes made through the lesson itself.

*AFTER THE LESSON*

1. You now have quite a detailed idea of the sort of decisions you have inferred the teacher made about the lesson during the planning phase. Discuss your inferences with the teacher. This may promote a very interesting discussion.
2. Actual lessons tend to vary in some degree from the pre-conceived plan. For this reason, teachers often debate the value of expending time and concentration in the planning phase.

Look at these hypothetical answers to the question: is it worth planning a lesson?

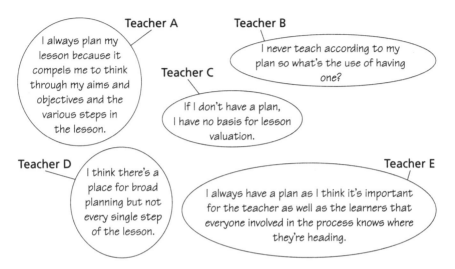

**Teacher A**
I always plan my lesson because it compels me to think through my aims and objectives and the various steps in the lesson.

**Teacher B**
I never teach according to my plan so what's the use of having one?

**Teacher C**
If I don't have a plan, I have no basis for lesson valuation.

**Teacher D**
I think there's a place for broad planning but not every single step of the lesson.

**Teacher E**
I always have a plan as I think it's important for the teacher as well as the learners that everyone involved in the process knows where they're heading.

With which of these answers do you feel comfortable?

What value(s) can be gained from lesson planning?

3. Many lesson plans used during training courses are idealised, in that they include far too much detail and require too much attention in the lesson. This can distract the teacher and may also create an unnecessary dependency on the plan or may encourage a rigid approach to teaching.

Design a lesson plan format that bridges the gap between the ideal and the real, and is one that you would use before the lesson (planning), during the lesson (checking/consulting) and after it (evaluating). You may wish to list the decisions to be made by the teacher as a set of questions.

## REFLECTION

Do you plan your lessons? If so, to what degree? Can you use the experience gained during this observation to refine and improve your planning procedures?

## ACKNOWLEDGEMENT

This observation is based on a teacher training workshop on lesson planning given by Jenny Hannan at the Sydney English Language Centre in 1989.

## 4.2 Openings and closures

### BACKGROUND

The basic unit of teaching, most would agree, is the lesson. Every lesson has a beginning and an ending, or an entrance and an exit. Of course it also has its own internal stages. There are certain predictable conventions or routines that accompany the entrance and exit stages of the lesson.

### TASK OBJECTIVE

The purpose of this task is to refine understanding of the conventional routines that characterise the start and end of a lesson, especially the purposes they serve. You will be observing sections of a number of lessons to collect data of what teachers do at the start and end of their lessons.

### PROCEDURE

*BEFORE THE LESSON*

1. Arrange to see the starts and ends of a number of lessons. (You might like to integrate this task with other tasks that you do, reserving the entrance and exit phases for this task.) Begin by defining for yourself what you understand to be an 'opening' and 'closure' of a lesson, and use these definitions to guide your data collection.
2. Prepare yourself by reflecting on what you yourself do to begin or end a lesson. How much of this is conscious? How much is 'ritualised'? Consider now what sort of items you might want to be alert to.
3. Make yourself familiar with the data collection chart opposite.

*DURING THE LESSON*

Use the chart to help you record data from about three lessons.

1. In the left-hand column record chunks of teacher language taken from different openings and closures.
2. Make a note of any non-verbal behaviours (e.g. eye contact, teacher manner) in the next column.
3. Analyse each opening/closure for its functional steps, that is, look at what happens in each one. Use the example in the chart for guidance.
4. Note whether the nature of the interactive pattern is: teacher-to-class (T–C), teacher-to-group of students (T–G) or teacher-to-student (T–S).

|  | Teacher language | Non-verbal signals | Teacher language analysed | Interactive pattern |
|---|---|---|---|---|
| **Opening 1** |  |  | T enters, chats to S<br>T socialises with group of SS<br>T greets whole class | T – S<br>T – G<br>T – C |
| **Closure 1** |  |  | T asks SS to stop work<br>T recaps lesson aims<br>T reminds SS re homework | T – C<br>T – C<br>T – C |

## 4 The lesson

1. In *Before the lesson* you defined for yourself what you understand by the opening and closure of a lesson. Looking at the data you have collected, do you think that your definitions are shared by the teachers you have observed? Would you now like to change or refine your definitions in any way?

2. While it is impossible and unwise to prescribe a fixed routine of opening or closing a lesson, try to draw up a broad paradigm of functional steps that characterise opening or closing a lesson. Put these roughly in the order you think most appropriate.

   The following comments and questions might guide you.

   *Openings*
   a) Is there any difference in the way a teacher speaks and behaves to one or two students and the way she or he addresses the whole class?
   b) How important is student exposure to natural language in genuine communicative situations such as a teacher greeting a student individually on entering the classroom?
   c) Is it important to link the coming lesson to other lessons, previous or forthcoming?
   d) Is it better to review previous work or plunge into new work?
   e) Is it important how students are feeling at the start of a lesson? How are the teacher's opening routines related to this?
   f) Do you think the teacher should tell the students what the coming lesson is about or have them induce this through discovery? What advantages/drawbacks accompany each strategy?

   *Closures*
   a) Signalling the end of a lesson with an abrupt 'Stop!' is clearly not a conducive way to wind down a lesson! How can a teacher ease the end of an activity into the end of a lesson?
   b) Is making space for questions from students a good way of closing a lesson?
   c) Is it important how students feel as they leave the classroom?
   d) Is it worthwhile to review the lesson's aims and content at the end of the lesson?
   e) Is it important to link this lesson with previous and coming ones? Why/why not? How might this be done?

3. To ensure that the routines of closure take place, enough time (but not too much) is needed at the end of the lesson. This is a question of timing, difficult to fix rigidly as lessons often need to deviate from set plans in order to follow and address student needs. What strategies can the teacher employ to try to maintain a space at the end of the lesson for adequate closure?

4. Maingay (1988) comments on the need to de-ritualise ritualised teaching behaviour. Sometimes this behaviour has become ritualised because it was first learned as unprincipled technique, that is, copied without having been fully understood. At other times, teaching can become ritualised through a lack of re-appraisal or reflection.

To what extent do you think entrances and exits into/from lessons and classrooms are prone to ritualisation?

## REFLECTION

It might be the case that your own routines for starting and ending a lesson have started to become ritualised. You may be able to gauge this to some extent by noting them down.

## 4.3 Lesson phases and transitions

### BACKGROUND

A lot of different events make up a lesson. These can be grouped into broad lesson stages, or into even smaller phases. How we divide them up very much depends on the criteria we use. Two major sets of criteria are: the purpose of the activity, such as accuracy versus fluency, and the means of organisation such as teacher-directed versus student-controlled (Byrne 1987).

How we recognise the end of one activity or phase and the start of another is usually through the teacher's signals. These links signpost, or 'frame', the steps of the lesson.

### TASK OBJECTIVE

In this observation you will refine your understanding of types of lesson activities as you explore the purposes behind various parts of the lesson. You will be observing classroom events from the perspective of points on a continuum, or more accurately, on two continua. One is a continuum measuring accuracy–fluency; the other measures the degree of teacher control or learner self-direction. As you observe the various events that happen in the lesson, you will consider where they belong on the continua.

In addition, you will be noting features of the lesson's cohesion – the ways a teacher signposts the steps in the lesson and links them together.

## PROCEDURE

1. Arrange to observe a lesson (or a number of lessons in sequence).
2. Make yourself familiar with Figure 4.1. Note that the horizontal axis runs from accuracy to fluency. The vertical axis runs from whole-class activities controlled by the teacher to small-group work, directed by the learners themselves. One way of understanding the vertical axis is to consider how much teacher control is required for the activity to take place.

   Here are some examples of activities:

   A: activities led by the teacher for the purpose of controlled language practice, e.g. drills, some types of games
   B: activities conducted by the learners, oriented to controlled language practice, e.g. practice of a model dialogue
   C: an activity led by the teacher, oriented towards fluency, e.g. a brainstorm activity where the teacher addresses the whole class and elicits ideas from them
   D: an activity controlled by the students, oriented towards fluency, e.g. a small-group, information-gap exercise requiring students to make choices in the language they use, rather than practise particular patterns exclusively (Byrne 1987).

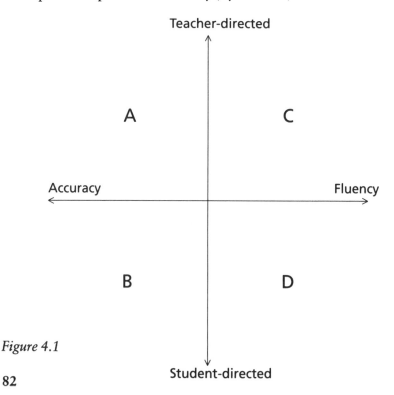

*Figure 4.1*

*DURING THE LESSON*

1.  As you observe the lesson, record the events in chronological order by marking them with a number and brief note in the appropriate sector of the grid: A, B, C or D. For example, '2' would indicate the second phase of the lesson, and 'drill' would identify the event. You may like to do this for the whole lesson or only for a portion of it.
2.  In this lesson you are also observing the teacher's signalling, that is, the signs given to indicate that one phase is over, and the next about to begin. Try to 'catch' about five such signals.

    Use Chart 4.3 to help you here. Record what the teacher said and did. Also note where in the lesson this happened: you could use your numbering system from Figure 4.1 to help you. The notes in the example given mean that the teacher clapped her hands and said 'right' loudly, and that this happened at the end of the second event and before the third.

| EX. no. | What did teacher say? | What did teacher do? | When / lesson phase |
|---|---|---|---|
| | 'Right - OK.' | Clapped hands | 2 → 3 |
| | | | |

4.3  Lesson phases and transitions

*AFTER THE LESSON*

1. Consider Figure 4.1 now that it is filled in with data. Take some time to re-consider where you have allocated various activities. Is there any entry that you now feel might be better placed in a different quarter from the one chosen? Did you have any difficulty in classifying classroom events/activities into one of the four segments? You may like to discuss this with the teacher and see to which degree you concur in your understanding of the purpose of each activity.
2. Examining your completed grid, do any patterns, tendencies or preponderances emerge? How did this manifest itself in the classroom?

   Consider factors like:

   – teacher/student talking time;
   – patterns of student interaction;
   – treatment of error;
   – roles of teachers/students.

3. If possible, select two entries on your grid that are very different, for example, a teacher-led accuracy-oriented activity and a student-led fluency-oriented activity. Comment, if possible, on the relationship between the teacher's role and teacher talk.
4. Looking now at the data you collected on signalling, what general patterns, if any, emerge, in the teacher's style of indicating stages in the lesson? Can you make a list of the various techniques open to a teacher to be used as signposting phases in a lesson?
5. Why is signalling important in teaching? What effect does it have on concentration? Does it have any influence on learner motivation and involvement in the lesson? How does it influence the flow and pace of a lesson?
6. There are some dangers involved in signalling: for example, the teacher's signals can intrude on learner space. Also, very directive signalling can be used to channel all student's energies into a lockstep classroom rhythm, that is, one based on whole-class activities directed by the teacher. Comment on these dangers and the warning symptoms.

## REFLECTION

Has the experience of observing this lesson resulted in your re-appraising any aspect of your own teaching? How might you take this further?

## 4.4 Grammar as lesson content

### BACKGROUND

There is perhaps no subject more hotly debated by language teachers than the place of grammar in language teaching (e.g. Prabhu 1987b; Rutherford 1987; Larsen-Freeman 1986; Richards and Rodgers 1986; Harmer 1987). Over the years this has swung with fashion, with the 'structural' approach replaced by the 'functional-notional' approach which itself led up to the 'communicative' era in which the focus was placed centrally on communication.

Some of the principal issues here have revolved around the teaching of form versus the teaching of meaning; the teaching of knowledge (competence) versus the teaching of skill (performance). And hovering over all of this is the question of how explicit and conscious grammar should be in the classroom learning of a foreign language.

A basic distinction in the teaching of grammar has been between the deductive and the inductive approaches. In a deductive approach, learners are taught rules and given specific information about the language, which they are then expected to apply when they use the language. In an inductive approach, such as the communicative one, learners are not taught grammatical rules directly or explicitly, but are left to induce the rules from their use of the language. The emphasis here is on the experience of the language rather than the formal presentation of language.

### TASK OBJECTIVE

In this task you will be looking at the place of grammar in a lesson, what is said about it, to what sorts of uses it is put in the lesson, and what this reveals about the teacher's views of language and language learning.

### PROCEDURE

*BEFORE THE LESSON*

Arrange to observe a lesson in which grammar will have some place. If possible, speak with the teacher in advance of the lesson, and discuss the lesson's aims in terms of its grammatical focus.

*DURING THE LESSON*

Keep an ethnographic record of the lesson. This means that you note down chronologically the main events in the lesson and their impact.

## 4 The lesson

This will have to be brief and synoptic enough for you to keep records 'in real time'. It does not have to include scripted actual language but rather a report of what was said and done. For example:

> T enters . . . greets whole class from the front of room. T announces what the lesson is going to be about today. T reminds SS how this lesson follows on from yesterday's . . . T drills new pattern . . . S asks question about the form of the verb in pattern on board . . . T explains. S seems to be satisfied but another S continues to ask similar question . . .

*AFTER THE LESSON*

For the purposes of the following questions, you should bear in mind your memory of the lesson and the specific contexts in which events occurred as well as your written narrative record of the lesson.

1. To what extent was an aspect of grammar the central focus of the lesson you observed?
2. Were the students consciously involved in thinking about grammar? Was a rule or rules presented to them or were they expected to work rules out for themselves? Were they helped or taught how to do this?
3. Describe the lesson in terms of the emphases on 'knowing' or 'doing': were the students finding out about how the language works or were they doing something with the language? Or both? And to what degrees?
4. If the students were at any time involved in doing something with the language, to what extent did the tasks or activities require them to make connections or inferences about the system of language?
5. Was there any evidence of a range of learning styles among the students in terms of how they reacted to a lesson involving grammar? Did these learning styles contrast with the teaching style in any way?
6. Have you any comments on the language used by the teacher to talk about language and how this facilitated access to understanding of the language?
7. Consider now any discussion about language that took place in the classroom, either among students, or involving the teacher. From the discussion, was there any evidence of learners trying to align new information with old – that is, processing recent input with their existing hypotheses about language?
8. Is it possible to summarise:

   a) what the students might have thought the lesson's objective was?
   b) what they came away with from the lesson?

Now contrast this with the lesson's objectives and its process.

Do you consider that it is important that students know what the lesson is going to be about and what objectives are set? Is it important that they come away from the lesson with what the teacher plans for them to come away with?

9. Considering the lesson you observed and the discussions you have had, what inferences can you draw from the lesson about (a) what language is, and (b) what language learning is to the teacher concerned? In other words, what theories (perhaps subconscious) underline the teacher's methodology? You may wish to pursue this in a discussion with the teacher.

10. In the debate about the place of grammar in teaching, one attempt to classify teaching according to the role of grammar is that proposed by Gibbons (1989) in his description of *focussed* versus *unfocussed instructional cycles*. Focussed instructional cycles have a particular language-item focus, such as a point of grammar, whereas unfocussed instructional cycles are more likely to be skills- or activity-based. You may wish to map this lesson that you have observed onto Gibbons's schemata in order to deepen your understanding of how grammar features.

## REFLECTION

Generally, what place does grammar play in your teaching? What does this say about what language and language learning are for you?

## 4.5 Lesson breakdowns

### BACKGROUND

A lesson breakdown, as the term is used here, is a very broad term for an interruption to a lesson, covering anything from minor hiccups to a major impasse. It is a point in a lesson when due to a communication problem or misunderstanding, the lesson is unable to proceed, whether for an individual or group of students or for the whole class. It can happen between teacher and student or in student–student interactions. And, of course, it may not happen at all! However, in all types of communication there is the potential for misunderstanding and therefore breakdown and repair. In the language learning classroom, where the target language being learned is *also* the medium of instruction, it is highly probable that breakdowns, small or large, will occur.

It is important to note that the term 'breakdown' is not a negatively-laden term and does not imply hostility or failure. Furthermore, the language used to negotiate the breakdown is itself meaningful and valuable and as such, constitutes an important source of real input for language learners. One might call it the very heart of the communicative classroom. Essential as it is to the processing of language, the learner's experience of the negotiation of meaning is integral to learning.

For example, in a lesson I observed, the teacher set up a paired activity as a prelude to a reported speech exercise involving the pattern 'What did s/he tell you?' After raising the topic of arguments and brainstorming a few typical topics of arguments, she then paired learners and set them up with the task of telling each other about their 'worst argument'.

The teacher expected the students then to get on with the task while she circulated among them and offered help as needed. However, quite a few pairs were unable to get started with the task as they were 'blocked' by two words:

— *argument*: was this a formal fight or could it be a domestic squabble? Was it only with words?
— *worst*: did this mean the loudest/most aggressive? Or the most important/serious in terms of topic? Or the most serious in terms of impact and result?

Mixed with the lexical confusion here was a cultural barrier as the concept of 'argument' varies from culture to culture.

The teacher then needed to address these issues before she could re-establish the paired activity and go ahead with the lesson as planned. The lesson's flow, then, was broken and needed repairing before it could resume course.

## TASK OBJECTIVE

This task is designed to allow you to collect some classroom data about lesson breakdowns. The data will then be analysed and discussed. We will be seeking to establish how the breakdown happened, and how, and by whom, it was resolved, if at all. In particular, we will be looking at the language used to negotiate and repair meaning; and considering the value of these aspects of the hidden agenda in the language classroom.

## PROCEDURE

*BEFORE THE LESSON*

1. Arrange to observe a class.
2. Make yourself familiar with the task and the chart opposite.

*DURING THE LESSON*

You are looking for evidence of any obstacles to the smooth flowing of the lesson. Use the chart below to help you collect a few instances of breakdowns. In each case:

1. Note what happened: what made it obvious that a breakdown was happening?
2. Trace the source of the breakdown.
3. Comment on the language used while meaning between teacher and students was negotiated and repair attempted or achieved.

| What happened? | Source of breakdown | Language used for repair and negotiation | Seriousness of breakdown |
|---|---|---|---|
|  |  |  |  |

4.5 Lesson breakdowns

*AFTER THE LESSON*

1. In the far right column of the chart categorise the instances of breakdown as 'minor' or 'major', where 'major' is defined as interrupting the smooth flow of the lesson.
2. In the case of the breakdowns you observed:

   – could the breakdown have been avoided altogether?
   – could it have been repaired more efficiently?

3. In the instances of breakdowns that you collected, consider:

   – the pattern of interaction at the time of a breakdown;
   – the language used by the teacher and students in the attempt to negotiate meaning and repair the breakdown.

   Now comment on the value that the experience and encounter might offer for the learner.

   In the light of the fact that breakdowns are a usual part of normal conversational/interactional language flow, how do we weigh up the value of the language experience for the learners versus the interruption to the smooth flow of the planned lesson?

4. In the face of a breakdown, what can a teacher do to:

   – heighten the value of the breakdown for all the class?
   – minimise the interrupting effect on the lesson?

## REFLECTION

How aware are you of breakdowns in your lessons and the language used to negotiate and repair meaning? Have you learned anything through this observation experience that you would like to pursue further?

## ACKNOWLEDGEMENT

I am grateful to Sylvia Skeffington for insights into this task.

# 5 Teaching skills and strategies

## 5.1 Presenting

### BACKGROUND

In recent years a lot of attention has been given to the varying roles that a language teacher has. Increasing emphasis has been placed on the less obtrusive roles such as monitoring language use and facilitating communication. In some versions of the communicative and task-based approaches there is often no formal presentation phase.

Nevertheless, even with the welcome increased focus on student talking time over teacher talking time, the skill of presenting remains a key one in the repertoire of a language teacher, as learners still often look to the teacher to perform this role.

### TASK OBJECTIVE

The objective of this task is to raise awareness of the key components of a successful presentation.

### PROCEDURE

*BEFORE THE LESSON*

1. This task involves you watching the presentation phase of a lesson. It may be of value to watch this in a number of different lessons.
2. Make yourself familiar with the chart and diagram.

*DURING THE LESSON*

1. During the lesson, record what happens by completing Chart 5.1. (Use a new chart for each lesson.) Record the chronological events in terms of what the teacher does and what the students do.
2. You may like to keep a record of teacher movement in or around the classroom. A convenient way of doing this is to make a diagram of the classroom (see Figures 5.1 and 5.2), and note the teacher's position with a cross, plus a note of the time.

| What teacher does | What learners do |
|---|---|
| *Greet/chat with SS* | *Greet/respond to T* |
| *Warm SS up by reminding them of yesterday's lesson* | *Recall yesterday's lesson* |

5.1  Presentation phase

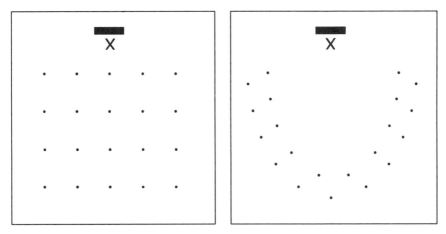

Figure 5.1                    Figure 5.2

AFTER THE LESSON

1. Using the data you have collected and your awareness of the effectiveness of the various parts of a presentation, prepare a list of the key components of a presentation. Discuss your list, along with your data of the lesson, with the teacher.

2. Considering your list of the various key components of a presentation, say what you believe to be the purpose of each.
3. A traditional part of the presentation of new language is the drill phase. What is meant by 'drill' here is the phase in which the students practise the language in a very controlled way under the close guidance of the teacher. The focus is necessarily limited and accuracy-oriented, yet not necessarily mechanical or meaningless.

   Is it important that the students understand the language – both its form and meaning – prior to the drill phase? What are the implications of drilling with or without attention to student understanding? What is revealed, in each case, about the teacher's approach to language learning?
4. One element of the presentation phase is the teacher's voice. A number of qualities are relevant here:

   - audibility;
   - projection;
   - speed;
   - clarity;
   - lack of distortion.

   What do you understand by each of these terms?
5. Another element of the presentation phase is the physical position of the teacher in the classroom. Consider now the notes you took regarding teacher position. What comments can you make about teacher position and movement?
6. Consider the presentation(s) you have observed in terms of the actual target language presented. What context was used to embed the language? How 'natural' do you consider the context to have been? Did the context 'naturally' generate the target language forms? Did it foster a learning link between language and situation?
7. Now consider the presentation mode used by the teacher to present new language. For example, was the language presented aurally via a tape recorder or visually, in written form?

   Consider the relationship between presentation mode and language form: was the mode appropriate to the language forms and the language register being presented?

## REFLECTION

Using these observations of presentations as a mirror of your own teaching, what comments can you make about your own presentation style and procedure? How did you acquire this style and procedure? How might you improve or refine them?

## 5.2 Eliciting: teacher prompts

### BACKGROUND

Teachers elicit for a range of reasons: to set students thinking in a certain direction; to steer them towards a certain pre-planned topic or lesson objective; to create a context; to warm a class up; to generate peer interaction/correction; to lead into an activity; to attract and focus attention; to increase student talking time; to allow the teacher to assess what is already known about a particular topic, structure or area of vocabulary; to draw out passive knowledge; and to tap into the students as a learning resource and engage them in the learning process.

### TASK OBJECTIVE

This observation task is designed to help you become aware of some important aspects of the skill of eliciting. You will consider types of question prompts, the amount of time the teacher allows, the kinds of responses elicited, and the general purposes that eliciting serves. A particular focus is the purpose of the eliciting and any link between purpose and question-type. (Other aspects of questions are dealt with in Task 2.2, *The language of questions.*)

### PROCEDURE

*BEFORE THE LESSON*

Arrange to observe a lesson in which some eliciting is planned. If possible, get a list of the possible prompts that the teacher plans to use.

*DURING THE LESSON*

Using Chart 5.2, record:

1. What the teacher says in order to elicit a response.
2. How much time the teacher allows before re-phrasing, or re-directing or adding a prompt (count the time in seconds and record it under *Wait time*).
3. What students offer as a response.

Record about five exchanges.

| Teacher prompts | Wait time | Student responses |
|---|---|---|
| 'Who can tell me where the Amazon is?' | / / / / | |
| 'Is it in Africa or South America?' | / / | 'In South America.' |

5.2 Eliciting: teacher prompts

*AFTER THE LESSON*

1. Consider the data you have collected. Is there any *pattern* in the language the teacher used? For example, are the following used: *open questions* ('What do you think of . . .?'); *closed questions* ('What's the word for . . .?'); *imperative prompts* ('Tell me what you know about . . .'); *directed questions* ('Anton, what can you tell me about . . .?')?

2. Do you think the type of pattern that the teacher uses has an *influence* on *whether* students respond? Or on *how* students respond? Can we link the question form with the notion of ease/difficulty? Can we link it to the form of the response? Consider, for example, binary questions (offering a choice of two answers) or open-ended questions.

3. What did you notice about *wait time*? Did this seem to influence students in any way? What did you notice about any subsequent re-formulations?

4. Consider the *purposes* that eliciting served in the lesson you watched. For each one of the entries you recorded under *Teacher prompts*,

consider what purpose was intended or achieved, for example, 'Who can tell me where the Amazon is?' might be used to lead into the topic of the lesson.

5. Is it possible to establish a link between:

   — the purpose of the question;
   — the form of the question;
   — the way the teacher responds to student response(s)?

6. Are there any times in a lesson when you think it is better for the teacher to *tell* the students rather than attempt to elicit something from them?

## REFLECTION

You may like to monitor your own eliciting patterns by recording some of your teaching. Contrast your predictions about your own eliciting with the data you collect.

## 5.3  Eliciting: teacher responses

### BACKGROUND

As Task 5.2 points out, eliciting is a teaching strategy that can have a range of purposes.

As important as the actual eliciting question prompt, is the teacher's response to what students offer. This is especially the case when the elicitation is designed to take the lesson towards a pre-planned point. One danger is that the questioning can become a guessing game about what's in the teacher's head!

Sometimes students give back exactly what the teacher is looking for; sometimes they don't. In the latter case, the teacher has a delicate balancing act to perform: to accept only those answers that move the lesson along as planned but to maintain a classroom atmosphere that encourages students to contribute and speak out without fear of rejection.

### TASK OBJECTIVE

This observation task is designed to help you find out more about patterns of teacher responses to learners in an elicitation context.

## PROCEDURE

*BEFORE THE LESSON*

1. Arrange to observe a lesson in which the teacher engages in some eliciting. If possible, speak to the teacher before the lesson and seek a list of possible prompts that the teacher plans to use.
2. Make yourself familiar with the chart overleaf.

*DURING THE LESSON*

1. Pay close attention to the eliciting prompts that the teacher uses and record them in the chart, under *Teacher prompt*.
2. In the next column, record how the student responds.
3. Then record the teacher's response to the student's response.
4. Make a note of any non-verbal signals (*N/V signals*) that accompany the teacher's verbal response.
   (Note: the last column, *A/R*, is to be used after the lesson.)
   Collect about five exchanges.

| Teacher prompt | Student response | Teacher response | N/V signals | A/R |
|---|---|---|---|---|
| ☹<br>'How does he feel?' | 'Sad.' | 'Mm, that's right.' | Pointing to face on board, nodding at S | A |

5.3 Eliciting: teacher responses

*AFTER THE LESSON*

1. Now consider carefully your record of the language and other signals the teacher used in responding to student responses. You may have noticed that the teacher responses do not necessarily fall into a neat pattern of 'accept' or 'reject'. Consider your record of teacher responses and mark them A ( = accept), R ( = reject), or A/R (partial accept, partial reject) in the last column on the chart. Discuss these findings with the teacher.
2. How important is the teacher's response to learners' contributions? How can a teacher respond positively to a contribution that is only partially correct? Is it possible to reject (part of) the response without rejecting the learner?
3. Consider the following:

   a) What do you notice about any A/R responses?
   b) Are you able to *generalise* about features of the teacher's responses?
   c) How might the students have *felt* during or at the end of the lesson?
   d) What effect did the *teacher's behaviour* (verbal and non-verbal) have on the students?

4. Are there times when a teacher ought to accept only the answer wanted, and times when any contribution is to be valued? How does this link up with the purpose of the eliciting?

## REFLECTION

What have you learned about effective teacher responses to student responses in an elicitation context? Using this observation task as a mirror to your own teaching, what application can you make to your own practices?

## ACKNOWLEDGEMENT

The material in this task is derived in part from work by Pauline Taylor.

## 5.4 Giving instructions

### BACKGROUND

A key time in the lesson is the transition period between one activity and another, especially when this entails the students moving from group, pair or individual work. These periods require clear instructions from the teacher to the students if the lesson is to flow smoothly and effectively.

### TASK OBJECTIVE

In this task we will be examining the language of instructions. This will involve both the choice of what to include and exclude, what 'accompaniments' are valuable, and what sequence is effective.

It might be useful to observe the same class at different stages of the term to see if the language of instruction-giving alters as the students become more familiar with the kinds of activities they are asked to do.

### PROCEDURE

*BEFORE THE LESSON*

If possible, have a look at a lesson plan for the lesson you will be observing. The plan need not be exhaustive, but you should have an idea of the stages of the lesson and any activities the students will be doing. Consider the lesson plan from the point of view of where you would *expect* instructions to be given. Now, having carefully read the activities planned, roughly script the instructions as you would give them. (Use the chart overleaf.)

*DURING THE LESSON*

1. Listen carefully for the teacher's instructions. Collect these by scripting them as accurately as you can, using the same chart.
2. Try to notice whether there was any visual support, modelling or concept-checking and whether the teacher had to repeat the instructions. Note also whether the instructions were understood. Note information of this kind in the *Comments* column.

| Phase of lesson | Predicted instructions | Scripted instructions | Comments |
|---|---|---|---|
|  |  |  |  |

## 5.4 Giving instructions

*AFTER THE LESSON*

1. To what extent did the instructions you predicted occur in the lesson? How were they different from what you scripted in advance?
2. Looking over the chunks of instructions you collected, what *patterns* or *tendencies* do you notice in the teacher's language? Is there any tendency towards 'foreigner talk', that is, the peculiarly modified language that native speakers teachers often assume in speaking to learners?
3. Take one of your recorded chunks of teacher language, and try to *reduce it to accommodate a lower level of learners*. Follow these steps:

   a) Underline the information that the students *must* know in order to do what is required of them.
   b) Make any necessary language adjustments to reduce the instructions for an elementary group of learners, for example, remove any surplus information, reduce any complex vocabulary and substitute simpler words.
   c) Consider whether at any point in the process some visual support might be provided to accompany the aural message.
   d) Order the instructions into a logical sequence.
   e) Identify the main sections of the instructions and write a question for each of these that would check comprehension. Now build these questions into the script.

f) Now evaluate the instructions. You might like to try them out on another teacher and evaluate them together.

4. What comments would you make on the features given below that would guide a teacher towards more effective instruction-giving? In each case, consider how the feature might serve to make a set of instructions more effective.

> Segmenting/pausing: the way the verbal message is segmented and the time between segments
> Voice qualities
> Attending behaviour: teacher's position, eye contact, movement
> Visual support
> Cueing to aid memory
> Modelling
> Concept questions

5. One possible paradigm for instruction-giving is as follows:

   i) Give signal to engage class's attention.
   ii) State briefly the overall nature of the task.
   iii) Organise seating/groups.
   iv) Give instructions.
   v) Signal to start.
   vi) Monitor understanding – repeat/re-phrase as necessary.

   a) Do you think (ii) above is necessary?
   b) Do you think the organisation in (iii) should happen before or after the instruction-giving?
   c) Is there ever a place, in your opinion, for giving out the instructions at different times? For example, instructions for first part of task → students do first part of task → signal → instructions for second part of task → students do second part of task, etc.
      When might this be called for? Are there any drawbacks?
   d) To what extent is this paradigm reflected in your own predicted instructions? Discuss points of similarity/difference.

6. Sometimes, scripted instructions seem rather dictatorial. In regard to this, Gower and Walters comment (1988:37):

The way you give instructions indicates the way you exercise control and your attitude to the group . . . generally students, even adults, would not appreciate you trying to be more polite. It would be time-wasting and slow things down and would involve you in more complicated language than they can readily understand.

What is your view?

7. How do you resolve the apparent conflict in these two pieces of advice:

   a) Instructions 'should generally be below the level of the language being taught' (Gower and Walters 1988:25).
   b) Learners 'usually understand at a higher level than they speak or write' (*ibid.*:41).

8. This task lends itself nicely to some *micro-teaching*. Here are some samples:

   a) Give instructions for listening to a presentation dialogue. Ask gist questions (names of the people talking, where they are, what they plan to do), and tell the students to check their answers in pairs.
   b) Give instructions that will lead on to a cued practice phase. Students will be working in pairs (A and B), with one card each, on which there will be cued questions and answers (invitations for weekend + responses). When they finish, swap and repeat.
   c) Give instructions for a free role-play: there are two groupings of people (reporters and villagers) and two phases to the task:

      - reporters get together to discuss their interview questions, villagers get together to discuss their attitudes about the issue;
      - class breaks up into about three groups (of five each): four villagers + one reporter, and proceeds with interviews.

## REFLECTION

Have you become more aware of the process of instruction-giving? If so, what specific aspect of the before/during/after the lesson activities in which you were involved helped you towards a better awareness? Does this reveal anything to you about your own learning style?

You may like to monitor your own instruction-giving by:

- taping a lesson;
- being observed by a colleague;
- monitoring very closely the immediate effect of your instructions.

## 5.5 Managing error

### BACKGROUND

If teachers corrected every language error made in their class, far too much classroom time would be given over to correction. This has negative implications in that it might reduce learner willingness to take risks and experiment.

Teachers necessarily differentiate between errors that require immediate attention and errors that are better ignored or treated in another way or at another time. This is one of the many choices a teacher makes in regard to learner error.

### TASK OBJECTIVE

This observation task is designed to help you become more aware of the issues involved in error management. You will be attending to learner error, noting down some examples, watching for how the teacher responds and noting whether correction is given and how.

### PROCEDURE

*BEFORE THE LESSON*

1. Arrange to see a lower-level lesson, preferably one with an oral/aural objective.
2. Make yourself familiar with the chart overleaf.

*DURING THE LESSON*

Use the chart to help you record some instances of learner error and teacher response. Try to capture about eight such instances.

1. Script the instance of learner error; this might be inaccurate or inappropriate language.
2. Note whether the teacher responded and if so, a brief note as to what was said or signalled.
3. Note down where roughly in the lesson it occurred. This is a prompt to help you recall it later.
4. Note whether there was a particular focus at that point of the lesson, for example, on accuracy or fluency.

| Learner error | Teacher response | Lesson phase | A/F |
|---|---|---|---|
| | | | |
| | | | |
| | | | |
| | | | |
| | | | |
| | | | |

## 5.5 Managing error

*AFTER THE LESSON*

1. Did you observe any pattern in the teacher's way of responding to learner error? Discuss with the teacher their rationale for managing error.
2. Looking over the eight instances you collected, is it possible to *distinguish* among them, or perhaps *rank* them in order of importance? Which were very important to correct and which perhaps might have been overlooked?
3. How did *other students* respond to a student's error and (where relevant) to the teacher's response? Was there any peer correction, or peer interaction or discussion of the error? If so, what did the teacher say or do to encourage this?
4. Were there any opportunities for the students to *self-correct*? If so, do you recall anything the teacher said or did to encourage self-correction?
5. Was there a link between the *amount* of error correction and the *focus* of the phase of the lesson?
6. When the focus of the lesson is on *fluency* there may be ways in which a teacher can avoid interrupting the flow of the students' language. Is error correction necessary at such times in a lesson? Is it possible to correct in a non-obtrusive way?
7. Was there any evidence in the lesson of students' *processing information*? For example, in committing an error, having it pointed out,

hearing the correct version and trying it out, a learner might simply be echoing what they think is required of them, or they might be *processing*, that is, adjusting existing notions or hypotheses about language to accommodate newly received information.

8. Focus on *the teacher's language* in response to an error. Were there any occasions when the teacher responded to the error without attending to *the student's intended meaning*, that is, attended exclusively to the form of the language?

What effect did this have: on the student? on other students? on the lesson?

## REFLECTION

What experience do you have of being corrected when speaking a second or foreign language? Do you think this has influenced your teaching?

Much, if not all, of what a teacher says and does in the classroom is a *reflection* of that teacher's belief (conscious or otherwise) about how people learn languages. Considering your own style of managing error, how does this reflect your underlying beliefs?

## ACKNOWLEDGEMENT

The material in this task is derived partly from work by Karen Smith.

# 6 Classroom management

## 6.1 Managing classroom communication: patterns of interaction

### BACKGROUND

This task is concerned generally with how communication takes place in a classroom setting, and specifically with the patterns of interaction that provide the vehicle for communication.

### TASK OBJECTIVE

In this task you will be collecting data about how communication is realised in the classroom, for example, who talks and to whom, who questions, who responds.

### PROCEDURE

*BEFORE THE LESSON*

1. Arrange to observe a lesson, preferably (but not essentially) one with a focus on oral–aural skills.
2. Make yourself familiar with Figure 6.1.

*DURING THE LESSON*

Use Figure 6.1 (based on Woodward 1991) to help you record information about the patterns of interaction that happen through the lesson.

1. Draw up a seating plan including students' names. This means that if students move from their seat during the lesson, their interactions can still be plotted onto the diagram.
2. Lines are drawn between the names of the people who are speaking to each other. Decide on symbols to represent different kinds of interactions: for example, a little arrowhead can indicate a nominated question (when the teacher is directing a question to a particular student); a return arrowhead can indicate a response.

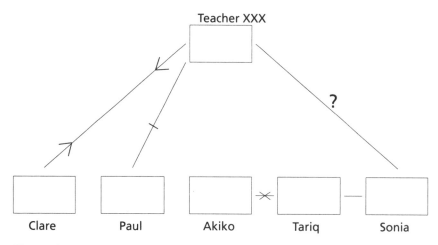

*Figure 6.1*

3. Start with marking in one type of interaction. As you develop the skill, work out symbols for other kinds of interaction patterns and plot them (most of the following symbols are from Woodward 1989). For example:

   – place an X next to the teacher when the question asked is open or undirected, e.g. 'Does anyone know . . .?' 'Who can tell me . . .?':

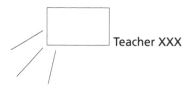

   – place a slash on the line when a student volunteers a response unprompted, e.g. Paul to T:

   – students interacting in pairs as directed, e.g. Akiko + Tariq:

  – students interacting without being directed, e.g. Tariq + Sonia:

  _____

  – questions asked by students, e.g. Sonia to T:

?

  _____

*AFTER THE LESSON*

1. Analyse the notes you have taken and make some summary statements of the overall patterns of interaction. Now confer with the
   teacher you observed and discuss the lesson and the communication
   patterns that have emerged.
2. If learning is all about re-appraising old concepts to accommodate
   new ones, to what extent do you think each of the types of patterns
   catered for in the diagram would be the most conducive to or
   facilitative of learning?
3. Clearly any lesson will contain a number of types of interaction.
   Consider different phases of lessons, different teacher roles and
   different activities in terms of which type of interaction is most
   appropriate. Is it possible to correlate certain interaction patterns as
   most suitable for certain lesson or activity types? For example, what
   type of interaction pattern characterises a student-centred
   information-gap activity, or a teacher correction phase following a
   role-play activity?
4. Much has been written about teacher-directed lockstep communication versus learner-based group work. Much has also been written
   about the value of group work. Apart from the obvious advantage of
   giving each student greater opportunity for 'air time', there are other
   advantages such as:

   a) A group of people is likely to be more reliable than any one
      individual when it comes to completing a task or activity.
   b) A correction from a peer is more telling because it comes from
      someone who has had the same amount of exposure to the
      language, and not from someone with professional qualifications.
   c) At the same time a correction from a peer is generally less
      threatening both because the one doing the correcting is not the
      person who gives out the grades, and because the correction is less
      likely to come in a judgemental tone of voice.

d) Competition between groups is less threatening to individuals than competition between individuals, and at the same time, equally exhilarating.

e) Group work requires risking and collaborating and is conducive to feelings of loyalty and group membership.

(This list is based on Stevick 1980:202.)

Can you add more?

One disadvantage for students that Stevick cites is 'having (their) mistakes less dependably corrected'. Can you list other disadvantages of group work?

Is there a compromise view that allows the teacher to marry the best of both lists?

## REFLECTION

Using this observed lesson as a mirror of your own teaching, what comments can you make about the patterns of communication that happen in your lessons? If there is anything you would want to change, how could you go about doing so?

## 6.2 Managing pair and group work

### BACKGROUND

Many classrooms these days involve a range of interactive patterns, using teacher-led activities, pair work and group work to varying degrees, depending on learning needs, purposes and contexts. Using a range of activities requires the teacher to move in and out of different interactive patterns smoothly and efficiently. Pair and group work also requires different teacher skills from those involved in teacher-led activities. Efficient transitions through the various lesson phases are integral to effective classroom management.

### TASK OBJECTIVE

This task will focus on the organisational skills involved in the transitions between activities, the characteristics of teacher intervention during pair or group work, and the management of information transfer, specifically in the report-back phase following pair or group work.

## PROCEDURE

*BEFORE THE LESSON*

1. Arrange to observe a lesson that will contain a range of interactive patterns.
2. Make yourself familiar with the chart so that you can use it effectively for taking notes on the various phases of the lesson.

*DURING THE LESSON*

Monitor the teacher's way of getting students in, through and out of activities. Try to record details of:

a) a moving-in phase
b) a monitoring phase
c) a moving-out phase.

*a) Moving into an activity*

Observe the teacher and comment on the following features:

i)   organising the groups and seating
ii)  giving instructions, including modelling and checking
iii) appointing and briefing group leaders.

*b) Monitoring pair/group work*

Observe the teacher and comment on the following features:

i)   how the teacher monitors
ii)  in what circumstances she or he speaks to a group
iii) the teacher's voice, position, proxemics (the distance between people who are conversing).

*c) Moving out of an activity*

Observe the teacher and comment on the following features:

i)   winding pairs/groups down
ii)  signalling for everyone's attention
iii) re-orienting group to new phase of lesson
iv)  organising and monitoring the report-back phase.

| | Sub-skill | Observation | Comment |
|---|---|---|---|
| **a) Moving into an activity** | i) Organising groups, seating, etc | *T selects group members.* | *T seems to be deliberately creating groups of mixed levels.* |
| | ii) Instructions | | |
| | iii) Appointing, briefing leaders | | |
| **b) Monitoring pair/group work** | i) Monitoring | | |
| | ii) Verbal contact | | |
| | iii) Teacher's voice, position, etc | | |
| **c) Moving out of an activity** | i) Winding down | | |
| | ii) Signalling | | |
| | iii) Re-orienting | | |
| | iv) Reporting back | | |

6.2  Managing pair and group work

*AFTER THE LESSON*

1. Discuss your notes with the teacher. Together, compile a list, in roughly chronological order of the various sub-skills involved in both moving into and out of an activity. Consider the purposes of each.
2. Consider the skill of teacher intervention during group work. Do you consider the following statements (based on Brown 1988:9) to be totally true or false, or partially true or false? Add any relevant comments or qualifications as necessary.

   a) A teacher monitoring a group is there to listen, help and monitor, but not to teach.
   b) Any teacher comment must be preceded by the teacher listening closely to the group to find out how they are getting on.
   c) Any interaction must be initiated by the group or its members but not by the teacher.
   d) The teacher must give equal time to the groups.
   e) The teacher must give equal time to individuals within the groups.
   f) The teacher must sit or crouch down so that she or he is at the same height as the students.
   g) Proxemics, eye contact and tone of voice in group work are necessarily different from those in full class activities.

3. There are different ways of grouping students. Recall the one used in the class you observed and consider it from the point of view of the group member. Consider the ease with which members of the pair or group were able to:

   – communicate;
   – relax, be comfortable;
   – concentrate on the activity;
   – see the board;
   – see/hear the teacher;
   – work silently;
   – be included as an equal member.

4. One way of organising report-back is to call on each of the group leaders to present their reports. Are there other ways? What are the advantages/disadvantages of each of these? Is there a correlation between task type and report-back style?

## REFLECTION

Of the various skills covered in this observation, which do you feel you would most like to consider further in relation to your own teaching?

## 6.3 Teaching and learning roles

### BACKGROUND

Within the time frame of any one lesson, there is a range of roles that a teacher may adopt, and a range of corresponding learner roles as well. An important aspect of effective teaching is the facility with which a teacher can move in and out of these various roles and enable learners to do likewise. This flexibility itself depends on the teacher's understanding of the purposes of different stages of a lesson and a clear sense of what the various corresponding roles of teachers and learners are (Wright 1987; Byrne 1987).

In a classic example of a *focussed instructional cycle* (Gibbons 1989), such as the Presentation–Practice–Production style of lesson, this may be depicted as in Figure 6.2. The size of the teacher's face per stage corresponds to the relative central focus of the teacher.

It is important to note that the order of the three 'P's may vary: sometimes, for example, in order to establish with clarity areas of need and motivation, the production stage may come before the presentation (see, for example, Woodward 1991: 195–7). Wherever in the lesson the production phase might occur, the relative and interconnected roles of teacher and learner would remain as facilitator/guide and producer/ communicator respectively.

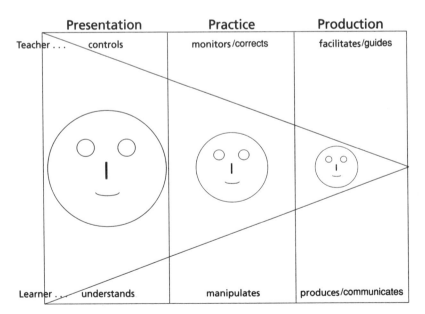

*Figure 6.2 is derived from a teacher training workshop given by Louise Austin at the Sydney English Language Centre in 1989.*

Another model which allows the roles of teacher to emerge very well is seen in Figure 6.3. Here each segment shows a facet of teaching and as you move in a clockwise direction you see a decrease in overt teacher 'face' as reflected in the degree of shading.

Of course, as with Figure 6.2, the various roles do not have to occur in the order shown. The actual sequence in which the various roles are adopted will depend on the lesson's plan, its objectives and processes.

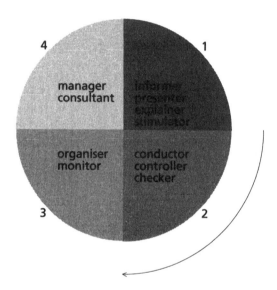

*Figure 6.3*

**TASK OBJECTIVE**

This task is designed to heighten your awareness of the various teacher roles and their corresponding learner roles.

**PROCEDURE**

*BEFORE THE LESSON*

1. Arrange to observe a lesson, and if possible obtain a copy of the teacher's lesson plan.
2. Study the plan and try to predict the kind of role the teacher will assume at each stage.
3. Consider the data collection chart on the following page.

*DURING THE LESSON*

Use Chart 6.3a to collect data from the lesson. As the lesson proceeds, note down information about the stage of the lesson, the teacher's role, and the corresponding learner's role. There is room in the far right column for any comments you wish to make.

| Lesson stage | Teacher's role | Learner's role | Comments |
|---|---|---|---|
|  |  |  |  |

6.3a  Teaching and learning roles

*AFTER THE LESSON*

1. Compare your predictions based on the plan you looked at before the lesson with the data you collected from the lesson.
2. Based on the lesson you observed, as well as your own experience as a teacher, what do you consider to be the major roles of teachers and learners?

   What overt behaviour would you associate with each role? Use Chart 6.3b to help you organise your thoughts.

| Teacher's role ► | Characteristic ► overt behaviour | Corresponding ► learner's role | Characteristic overt behaviour |
|---|---|---|---|
|  |  |  |  |

6.3b  Teacher and learner role behaviour

3. Were there any instances during the lesson when any learners did not behave in the expected learner role?

Have you experienced this in your own teaching?

To what factors may this behaviour be attributed?

What skills in classroom management are needed during such 'breakdowns'?

4. Do different lesson types (as defined by both objectives and activities) make different demands on the teacher and learners in regard to roles?

5. How do you think a teacher can gain greater facility in switching roles during a lesson?

## REFLECTION

What have you learned from this observation and consideration of roles that might benefit your own teaching?

## 6.4  Timing and pace

### BACKGROUND

The fact that teaching is itself a contrivance, an event that is structured and planned, means that it is in its very nature a process affected by the parameters and constraints of time.

The basic unit of teaching is 'the lesson'. This may vary in length depending on any number of factors, like the age of the learners, the intensity of the learning programme, other subjects being taught, timetable constraints within the school or learning context, etc.

When teachers are being trained, they are often advised to plan the timing factor of their lessons very carefully. This often proves quite difficult as beginning teachers are not yet adept at predicting the time an activity or phase of a lesson will last. They also have less control in terms of keeping a lesson 'on course' or following sidetracks judiciously. With more experience, teachers become more adept at planning the time and more able during the lesson to make judicious choices that affect the timing.

The initial planning concerning a lesson's timing, combined with spontaneous decision-making in the course of the lesson, add up to what we call a lesson's 'pace'. Pace is crucial in keeping students alert, motivated, engaged and 'on course'.

## TASK OBJECTIVE

This task aims to have you contrast timing at the planning phase (the lesson as planned) and timing at the phase of actualisation (the lesson as taught).

## PROCEDURE

*BEFORE THE LESSON*

1. Arrange to observe a lesson. You will need to meet with the teacher beforehand and discuss the lesson planned. Specifically ask the teacher about how the time has been planned, and how much time is expected per phase of the lesson. Ask for a copy of the lesson with the timing marked.
2. Fill in the relevant parts of the chart below.

| Lesson plan phases | Time planned | Actual lesson phases | Actual time spent |
|---|---|---|---|
|  |  |  |  |

6.4 Timing and pace

*DURING THE LESSON*

1. Observe the lesson from the point of view of *time spent* as contrasted with *time planned*. Keep notes on what happened during the lesson to explain changes from the lesson as planned.
2. While completing Step 1, also do a case study of one student in the classroom. As unobtrusively as possible try to chart the chosen student through the phases of the lesson. Comment on that student's ability to keep abreast of the lesson, or to stay in tune without lagging behind or becoming bored or restless.

*AFTER THE LESSON*

1. Discuss with the teacher the predicted versus the actual lesson timing. In particular, discuss those sections of the lesson which departed markedly from the plan, for example, parts omitted or different parts inserted. Discuss reasons for making these on-the-spot decisions, how the lesson varied as a result, the impact on learning, etc.
2. How closely did the actual lesson match the predicted one? Does it matter either way? If not, is there any purpose then in the planning phase?
3. Considering decisions made by the teacher in either the planning or the delivery phase, is there anything you would have done differently? Elaborate on the assumptions and reasons underlying this.
4. Given the definition of pace at the beginning of this task, what comment would you make on the pace of the lesson observed? What factors are relevant here?
5. Consider the number of times there was a switch of focus or activity in the lesson you observed. How did this affect the pace?
6. Focus now on the case study you recorded during the lesson. What external signs did the student give of keeping up with the pace? In the light of this, what comments would you make about how a teacher gauges whether it is time to move on, time to be silent and create 'space', time to revise and consolidate, etc.
7. Students who are rushed along too fast can have a range of negative responses: they might become distressed, angry or depressed; they might react by turning off to the lesson. Students whose learning pace is faster than the pace of lesson are prone to becoming bored, losing motivation and tuning out of the lesson.

   How can a teacher maintain a pace that caters for a mixture of language levels and learning pace?

## REFLECTION

Are you satisfied with the timing and pace elements of your own lessons? Is there any way in which you think these might be fine-tuned?

## 6.5 Classroom power

### BACKGROUND

Traditionally we think of the classroom as the place where the teacher 'knows' and the students 'don't know' and their reason for being there is to 'find out'. This model of education invests a great deal of power in teachers, many of whom assume that classroom power, as well as the responsibility for learning success, are fixed in their hands (Deller 1990; Leather and Rinvolucri 1989). In recent years this approach has been viewed with less and less favour by language teachers as they experiment with learner-centred teaching and skills-based learning.

### TASK OBJECTIVE

This task aims to have you reflect on:

— the many decisions that are made about learning, in and out of the classroom;
— who makes these decisions;
— the 'balance of power' that is the most effective in terms of learning goals.

### PROCEDURE

*BEFORE THE LESSON*

1. Arrange to observe a lesson. If possible, speak to the teacher before the lesson and ideally, discuss with the teacher the plan for the lesson, the aims, and any tasks or materials that are going to be used. Ask the teacher the first four questions in the list overleaf.
2. Now make yourself familiar with the rest of the questions in the list (adapted from Deller 1990:6).

*DURING THE LESSON*

Observe the lesson from the points of view of the questions in the list. As responses, write T ( = teacher), S ( = student) or T/S ( = a mixture of T and S) next to the questions.

Don't be concerned to capture every instance of the lesson – a rough indication is perfectly adequate.

## 6 Classroom management

1 Who chose the aims?
2 Who chose the language and/or skills focus?
3 Who chose the topic(s) and activities?
4 Who chose and prepared the materials?
5 Who chose the seating arrangements?
6 Who wrote on the board?
7 Who cleaned the board?
8 Whom did the students speak to?
9 Who created the pairs or groups?
10 Who decided when to stop an activity?
11 Who operated the equipment?
12 Who decided which questions or problems in the lesson were explored?
13 Who chose the vocabulary to be learned?
14 Who gave meaning for words?
15 Who spelled out new words?
16 Who gave explanations?
17 Who asked questions?
18 Who answered student questions?
19 Who repeated what was said if others didn't hear it?
20 Who created the silences?
21 Who broke the silences?
22 Who checked the work?
23 Who chose the homework?

*AFTER THE LESSON*

1. Based on your answers to these questions, what general tendencies can you point to in the lesson that you observed? Does this surprise you? Does it confirm your expectations?
2. While the overriding (if tacit) question during this lesson was 'Who holds the power?', a lot of ground was covered by the list of questions. You might like to select some discrete areas among the list of questions and then ask a new question: 'What value is there in having students, rather than the teacher, do X . . .?' For example:
   2. What value is there in having students choose the topics in a lesson?
   5. What value is there in having students organise the seating?
   6. What value is there in having students do some of the writing on the board?
   23. What value is there in having students decide on their own homework?
3. Consider more closely Questions 12, 16, 18 and 19. One thing these each have in common is that they concentrate on language used by the student during the lesson.

Consider the language that might be used in the classroom if students were given opportunities to: explore issues of their own choices and interest; give their own explanations of language as they understand it; answer some of each other's questions; repeat for their peers (and clarify? and make intelligible?) language used in the classroom.

4. What does 'a shift in power' imply for the roles of teachers and learners? How will this, in your opinion, affect learning processes and possible outcomes?

5. Many teachers are loath to 'let go' some of the crucial decision-making in their teaching. How do you account for this? What reasons might they give?

6. Handing over some decision-making power in the learning process to the learners certainly involves some risk, in that less of the lesson is predictable, less can be planned, more is spontaneous (Wajnryb 1992). What risks do you see in this process?

7. It might well be argued that we have a cross-cultural issue here: many students expect the teacher to hold all the decision-making power about the learning process. How might they react if some of this power were offered to them? If there is a clash of expectations, and especially if this is culture-bound, what strategies do you think might help here?

8. Deller (1990:1) writes: 'Our unsung trainers are our learners. They are the really powerful influence on our "on the job" development.'

   How do you think teaching with learner-generated material might be a source of development for the teacher?

## REFLECTION

Often when we observe someone teaching, the very process of observation stimulates self-reflection, as if observing were a kind of mirroring. Can you predict what sort of tendencies would emerge out of a lesson *you yourself* taught?

You may wish to respond to the questionnaire again, this time using your own teaching as the source of data.

What aspect of classroom decision-making would you like to share with learners? What risks or difficulties do you foresee in putting this into practice in your own classroom?

# 7 Materials and resources

## 7.1 The board as resource

### BACKGROUND

Language teaching varies dramatically around the world, but a board is usually an integral part of the language classroom.

### TASK OBJECTIVE

This task aims to have you consider how the resource of the board may be best exploited. You will gather information about the ways in which and the purposes for which the board was used in the lesson and use these to discuss related issues after the lesson.

### PROCEDURE

*BEFORE THE LESSON*

1. Arrange to see a lesson. If possible, find out the lesson's objective(s) and, ideally, obtain a copy of the lesson plan.
2. From what you find out in advance about the lesson, predict:

   - what you think the board might be used for;
   - how the board might be used.

*DURING THE LESSON*

1. At three points during the lesson copy the board's contents and layout exactly.
2. Take field notes about what happens while the board is being written on.

*AFTER THE LESSON*

1. Discuss the lesson with the teacher, sharing your notes and the three board replicas you took during the lesson. Discuss the decisions made about layout and board use. Would you have used the board differently? How? Discuss this too with the teacher.

2. The board may be used for a range of purposes, for example, teaching vocabulary, explaining grammar, drawing pictures, etc. Even within these categories, there may be sub-divisions, for example, drawing might be used to set a scene, to depict an action or to elicit vocabulary.

    Consider the *range* of purposes for which the board was used in the lesson you observed. Now create appropriate categories and sub-categories, for example:

3. Analysing the data you have collected from the lesson, would you say the board was used randomly or systematically, or somewhere in between these two? If you detected a system to the board use, describe it and evaluate its effectiveness.

4. A system often recommended for board use classifies things into three categories, based on their importance to the lesson and the time they are left on view:

    a) *reference* material: this is a permanent record of the lesson (to be left on display for the duration);

    b) material related to the *development of the lesson*: this tends to be cumulative and serves its main purpose at the time at which it is written up; it may be erased or transferred to the permanent section;

    c) the *unpredictable*, impromptu side of teaching, including odd 'perishables' and impromptu notes.

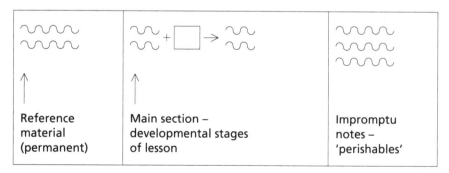

7.1 The board as resource

What comment can you make on this system? Do you recommend it, or aspects of it? Is there another system that you prefer?

5. Other aspects of board use that you might like to consider are:

   — *Who* writes on the board? Predominantly the teacher? Is there a place for students using the board? Is there a danger?
   — What happens in the lesson *while* the teacher (or someone else) is using the board? Use your field notes to help you answer this.
   — The legibility and comprehensibility of items on the board.

6. Now, having observed a lesson from the point of view of board use and having considered the board from a number of different perspectives, is there a place for some 'golden guidelines' that might help maximise the board as a teaching/learning resource? For example:

   — Start the lesson with a clean board to avoid the distraction of 'left-overs' from a previous lesson.
   — Avoid writing with your back to the class for long periods.

## REFLECTION

Reflecting on this lesson from the perspective of your own teaching, is there any particular aspect about board use that you would like to work on or explore further?

## 7.2 The learner as resource

### BACKGROUND

It has become a maxim of education to acknowledge that the greatest resource the teacher has is the learners themselves. This is especially important in the field of language teaching where the danger is that because one learns to use a language by using it, learner passivity and non-involvement will in fact sabotage outcomes. If the processes actively engage the learners, then a more positive outcome is assured.

### TASK OBJECTIVE

The objective of this task is to increase awareness of the diverse ways in which the learner may become a resource in the processes of learning.

### PROCEDURE

*BEFORE THE LESSON*

1. Arrange to observe a lesson.
2. Make yourself familiar with the data collection chart opposite.

*DURING THE LESSON*

1. Observe the lesson from the point of view of the learner's involvement.
2. Using the chart, record the times in the lesson when the learner is used as a resource, with details of the phase of the lesson so that you will be able to pinpoint each occasion later.
3. Comment on the process effect (what did it involve the learner(s) doing?) and perhaps later, at the end of the lesson, comment on the outcome effect (what was the result of involving the students in this way?). It is worth noting that as outcomes relate to learning, they may not be directly observable, and therefore your comments may be speculative.
4. As well as recording what happened in the lesson from the point of view of the learner's involvement, consider, too, points in the lesson where the learner was not involved but might have been. In a different coloured pen, perhaps, record how you think the learner might have been used as a resource, at which phase of the lesson, and predict what the process and outcome effects might have been.

| Learner as resource | Lesson phase | Process effect | Outcome effect |
|---|---|---|---|
|  |  |  |  |

7.2 The learner as resource

*AFTER THE LESSON*

1. Consider the data that you have collected from the lesson about when the learner was used as a resource. What patterns, if any, emerge? What comments can you make that are based on the data? Discuss the data with the teacher.
2. What *benefits* are to be gained from exploiting the learner as a resource? List these and classify them in a way that is meaningful to you.
3. Consider the phases in the lesson where you noted that the learner might have been used as a resource but in fact was not. Discuss this with the teacher. Consider the teacher's reasons for making these choices.

   Consider reasons for *not* involving the learner at certain times of a lesson. Consider the *precautions* that a teacher might need to consider before engaging the learner as a resource.
4. Focus now on the *process* effect that comes from involving the learner as a resource. What is the relevance of the notes you have made in Column 3 to factors involved in successful language learning? Similarly, consider the outcome effects.
5. How does the active involvement of learners as a resource affect the nature of teacher and learner roles in the classroom?
6. Is there any clash in the notion of active involvement on the one hand, and respect for culture-specific learning styles on the other? Is a compromise position possible?

## REFLECTION

To what extent is the learner regarded as a resource in your own teaching? In which ways do you currently avail yourself of this resource? In which ways might you explore future possibilities?

## 7.3 'Whole-learner' materials

### BACKGROUND

The concepts underlying this task derive from Stevick's notion of humanistic language teaching, in particular his criteria for the choice of what he calls 'whole-learner' materials (Stevick 1980).

Stevick believes that the adult language learner has to be treated as a complete person, not seen in exclusively cognitive terms. He puts forward six essential criteria for materials choice or development that allows the learning process to be personally meaningful to the learner. These are paraphrased as follows:

1. The material should be expressed in *language* that has some currency outside the classroom, language that resembles that used by and among native speakers.
2. The material should treat *the world and reality* as the learner knows them to be, not through some sterilising filter. The material, for example, should take good advantage of the adult learner's rich knowledge of the world.
3. The material should contain something of intrinsic interest for the *affective* side of the learner. Ideally, learners should be able to relate experientially to the material in some way.
4. There should be *a basis for disagreement* allowing the learner to make *choices*. Most groups of adults talking would reveal differences of opinion. Materials have to cultivate this factor, not avoid it or shut it down.
5. The material should allow learners to engage in *meaningful interaction* with one another. This means interaction where there is a communicative purpose, not mechanical repetition or perfunctory talk attending to form and not meaning.
6. The design of the material should contribute to the learner's sense of *safety or security in the learning context*. The learner has to know that the environment will allow for, even encourage, error-making. There can be no risk of humiliation in linguistic production or any other area. Part of this relates to human resource management, but it can also be a factor promoted in the materials themselves.

## TASK OBJECTIVE

This task asks you to reflect on Stevick's materials criteria and then to measure a lesson that you observe against them. Note that the focus here is on materials rather than method.

## PROCEDURE

*BEFORE THE LESSON*

1. Arrange to observe a lesson.
2. Make yourself familiar with Stevick's criteria, as described above, and the chart overleaf for use in the lesson.

*DURING THE LESSON*

Observe the lesson from the perspective of Stevick's criteria and make notes about the materials used during the lesson under the headings in the chart.

| Criteria | Your observations of the materials |
|---|---|
| The language of the materials | |
| 'Reality' as reflected by the materials | |
| Appeal to the learner's 'affect' | |
| Scope for choice/ disagreement | |
| Quality of students' interaction | |
| Safety of the learning environment | |

## 7.3 'Whole-learner' materials

*AFTER THE LESSON*

1. Evaluate the lesson in terms of the six criteria that Stevick puts forward. Specifically, to what extent:

   a) was the material expressed in 'real' language?
   b) was external reality fairly reflected?
   c) was the affective side of the learner catered for?
   d) was there a choice-generated basis for disagreement?
   e) was student interaction non-perfunctory?
   f) did the material contribute to a 'safe environment'?

   Share this exercise with the teacher of the lesson.

2. Now, having used each of the criteria as a measure for a lesson, assess the criteria themselves, one by one.

   To what extent do Stevick's criteria for materials match your own?

Which of the criteria do you take into consideration when you prepare or choose materials? What does this reflect of your theory of what language is and how people learn languages?

3. Humanistic language teaching principles tend to emphasise the individuality of the learner in contrast to behaviourist techniques which are more likely to impose a blanket conformity on a learning group.

There is a possibility, however, that there may be a type of cultural imperialism going on here, in that the focus on the individual may itself be considered a Western cultural concept. Imposed on peoples of a different culture base, this approach may lead to conflict rather than harmony, and it might lead in reality to disengagement from rather than engagement in learning.

Widdowson (1990:13): 'Individuality is itself a cultural concept; there can be no private independent real person disassociated from the cultural values which define the society in which the individual lives.'

Even imposed on people of a similar cultural base, it may be that the attention to the individual in humanistic language teaching is seen as an 'unwarranted intrusion on privacy'.

What experience can you bring to bear to support or counter these concepts?

## REFLECTION

How 'whole-learner' are the materials you tend to use? To what extent would you wish to be guided by the criteria Stevick proposes?

## 7.4 Task analysis

### BACKGROUND

Language lessons very often involve students 'doing' something with language, with some phases of the lesson involving specific tasks. For the moment, we will define a task as a piece of meaning-focussed work involving learners in comprehending, producing or interacting in the target language (Nunan 1989).

One way by which we can analyse a task is through the following framework, proposed by Nunan, of goal, input, activity, roles and setting.

An example of a task analysed using this framework is shown below. Students were given a questionnaire on sleeping habits. They had to make sure of the meaning and pronunciation of words and, following this, they had to use the questionnaire in paired interviews.

> *Goal*: exchanging personal information
> *Input*: questionnaire on sleeping habits
> *Activity*: i) reading questionnaire
> ii) asking/answering questions on sleeping habits
> *Teacher role*: monitor, facilitator
> *Learner role*: conversational partner
> *Setting*: classroom, pair work

(Nunan 1989:48)

## TASK OBJECTIVE

The objective in this observation is to help you to consider the various components of a language learning task.

## PROCEDURE

### BEFORE THE LESSON

1. Make yourself familiar with the framework for task analysis as given above. Arrange to observe a lesson that has a communicative goal and that will involve the learners using the language communicatively.
2. Make yourself familiar with the chart opposite.

### DURING THE LESSON

Use the chart to help you record information about a task used in the lesson. In the column *Observations*, make notes in regard to each of the task component headings.

| Task components | | Observations |
|---|---|---|
| Goal | = intended outcome(s) | |
| Input | = data that forms the point of departure of the task | |
| Activity(ies) | = what the learners are asked to do with the input | |
| Teacher role<br>Learner role | = the parts played in carrying out the task | |
| Setting | = the social arrangements in which the task is carried out | |

7.4 Task analysis

*AFTER THE LESSON*

1. How easy or difficult was it to analyse the task according to the categories of goal, input, activity, roles and setting? Would you like to *modify* these components in any way?
2. You may like to express your revisions *diagrammatically*:

a

learning task

3. In the light of your experience of observing and analysing a learning task, you may wish to reflect on the *definition* of 'task' (Nunan 1989), quoted on page 129. For example, consider these questions:

   a) Do you consider that a learning task always has to be meaning-focussed?

b) How important is it that a task involves the production of language?
c) Does a communicative task entirely preclude the use of the learner's first language?
d) To what extent should the task involve the learner in 'real-world' (not only classroom) activities/skills?
e) To what extent should the task be able to stand alone as an independent communicative act?

## REFLECTION

Make a note of what you consider you have learned through this observation. Looking to the future, do you predict any changes in the way you will be selecting/designing learning tasks? Are there any issues that you are interested in exploring further?

## ACKNOWLEDGEMENT

This task makes use of material in D. Nunan, *Designing Tasks for the Communicative Classroom*, Cambridge University Press, 1989.

## 7.5   Task design and evaluation

### BACKGROUND

This task seeks to identify and explore the features of a good language task. It also seeks objective ways of measuring classroom tasks in order to evaluate their effectiveness as materials. What criteria can be used to evaluate and design good learning tasks?

### TASK OBJECTIVE

You will consider your own criteria for the evaluation of good learning tasks; then evaluate a task in terms of these criteria; and then re-assess the original criteria.

## PROCEDURE

*BEFORE THE LESSON*

1. By way of preparation, consider your own beliefs about learning tasks. Consider the following six statements relating to the features of good learning tasks and circle the appropriate number on this scale:

0 - not a characteristic of a good task
1 - this characteristic is optional
2 - this characteristic is reasonably important
3 - this characteristic is extremely important
4 - this characteristic is essential

**Statements**

Good learning tasks should:

a) enable learners to manipulate and practise specific features of the
   language. ( 0 / 1 / 2 / 3 / 4 )

b) provide an opportunity for learners to rehearse communicative skills
   they will need in the real world. ( 0 / 1 / 2 / 3 / 4 )

c) involve learners in risk-taking. ( 0 / 1 / 2 / 3 / 4 )

d) involve learners in problem-solving or resolution. ( 0 / 1 / 2 / 3 / 4 )

e) be process - as well as product-orientated. ( 0 / 1 / 2 / 3 / 4 )

f) offer learners choice. ( 0 / 1 / 2 / 3 / 4 )

Are there any other characteristics that you would consider essential to a good learning task?

2. Now make yourself familiar with the questions to guide you during the lesson (see below).

*DURING THE LESSON*

1. Observe a complete lesson and pay particular attention to any learning tasks that the teacher sets. Consider the context of the task: how it is managed from beginning to end by the teacher; and how it is 'processed' by the learners.

2. Try to sit closely enough to be able to hear students working with a task. Listen for the language they produce to help them negotiate their way through the task.
3. Select *one* of these tasks and record information about the following aspects, using the questions below to guide you.

*Observing the teacher*

a) How was the task introduced?
b) What instructions were given?
c) How many steps were involved in the task?
d) Was any monitoring involved?
e) Was there a report-back phase?
f) How was the task 'resolved'?

*Observing the learners*

a) Was the level of the task commensurate with the level of the learners?
b) Were the instructions adequate for the task?
c) Were the learners able to 'process' the task?
d) Were the learners able to 'perform' the task?
e) Was collaboration/interaction involved?
f) Comment on the language of 'task-doing' that you overheard.

*AFTER THE LESSON*

1. Which of the tasks that you observed worked well and which didn't? Can you isolate the factors that are responsible?
2. Consider one task:

a) Was the task personally meaningful/relevant to the learners?
b) How many phases were involved?
c) How well did the learners cope with the 'logistics' of the task?
d) How complex were the instructions?
e) How much prior knowledge was assumed? Was this linguistic knowledge or knowledge of the world?
f) Were the language demands on the learner in line with their level of learning?

3. Return now to your pre-lesson activity. To what extent were the characteristics of a good learning task as you understand this apparent in the tasks you observed in the lesson?
4. You may wish to revise the list of criteria by which a good learning task can be evaluated (see *Before the lesson*). Are there any other features of a good learning task that you now wish to include? Are there any you now consider unimportant? Can you pinpoint any-

thing specific in the lesson that stimulated you to refine your understanding of tasks?

5. We have been looking at task design and choice. Consider now the question of management. How were the tasks managed?

   – By the teacher: consider how the tasks were introduced, what instructions were given, what monitoring took place and what round-off, report-back or resolution was involved.
   – By the learners: could they process the instructions? Perform the task as required? Were they comfortable with the climate of the task?

6. Consider the learners' language as they performed the task. In pair or group work, was language used to negotiate and collaborate? Was this related to the actual language needed to complete the task? How important is it that language is used to process and deal with the task?

## REFLECTION

Is there any aspect of your own task selection/design that you predict will change as a result of the experience of this observation task? If so, describe the change you predict.

## ACKNOWLEDGEMENT

This task draws ideas and material from D. Nunan, *Designing Tasks for the Communicative Classroom*, Cambridge University Press, 1989: 138–41.

# Bibliography

Abramson, L.V., Seligman, M.E.P., & Teasdale, J.D. (1978). Learned helplessness in humans: critique and reformulation. *Journal of Abnormal Psychology*, 87, 49–74.

Allwright, D. (1988). Each lesson is a different lesson for every learner. Paper given at 6th ATESOL Summer School, Sydney.

Alptekin, C. & M. (1990). The question of culture: EFL in non-English speaking countries. In Rossner, R. & Bolitho, R. (eds.), *Currents of Change in English Language Teaching*. Oxford: Oxford University Press.

Austin, L. (1990). Mixed levels: a two-pronged approach. *ELICOS ASSO-CIATION Journal*, 8, 2.

Bartlett, L. (1990). Teacher development through reflective teaching. In Richards, J.C. & Nunan, D. (eds.), *Second Language Teacher Education*. New York: Cambridge University Press.

Brown, R. (1989). Classroom pedagogics – a syllabus for the interactive stage? *The Teacher Trainer*, 2, 2 13–17; 3, 8–9.

Byrne, D. (1987). *Techniques for Classroom Interaction*. New York: Longman.

Deller, S. (1990). *Lessons from the Learner*. Harlow, UK: Pilgrim Longman.

Doughty, C. & Pica, T. (1986). 'Information gap' tasks: do they facilitate second language acquisition? *TESOL Quarterly*, 20, 2, 305–25.

Dulay, H., Burt, M., & Krashen, S. (1982). *Language Two*. New York: Oxford University Press.

Edge, J. (1989). *Mistakes and Correction*. New York: Longman.

Ellis, R. (1990). Activities and procedures for teacher training. In Rossner, R. & Bolitho, R. (eds.), *Currents of Change in English Language Teaching*. Oxford: Oxford University Press.

Fanselow, J.F. (1990). 'Let's see': contrasting conversations about teaching. In Richards, J.C. & Nunan, D., (eds.), *Second Language Teacher Education*. New York: Cambridge University Press.

Freeman, D. (1989). Learning to teach: four instructional patterns in language teacher education. *Prospect*, 4, 2.

Freire, P. (1970). *Pedagogy of the Oppressed*. New York: Seabury Press.

Gardner, R.C. & Lambert, W.E. (1972). *Attitudes and Motivation in Second-language Learning*. Rowley, Mass.: Newbury House.

Gebhard, J.G. (1990). Models of supervision: choices. In Richards, J.C. & Nunan, D. (eds.), *Second Language Teacher Education*. New York: Cambridge University Press.

Gibbons, J. (1989). Instructional cycles. *English Teaching Forum*, 27, 3, 6–11.

Giles, H. & Byrne, J.L. (1982). An intergroup approach to second language acquisition. *Journal of Multilingual and Multicultural Development*, 3,1.

Gower, R., (1988). Are trainees human? In Duff, T. (ed.), *Explorations in Teacher Training – Problems and Issues*. Harlow, UK: Longman.

Gower, R. & Walters, S. (1988) *Teaching Practice Handbook*. Heinemann.

Harmer, J. (1987). *Teaching and Learning Grammar*. New York: Longman.

Ingram, D. (1981). The on-going program: a methodological base paper for the Adult Migrant Education Program (Australia).

Larsen-Freeman, D. (1986). *Techniques and Principles in Language Teaching*. New York: Oxford University Press.

Leather, S. & Rinvolucri, M. (1989). Letting go of your power. *Practical English Teacher*, 10, 1.

Lindstromberg, S. (1988). Teacher echoing. *The Teacher Trainer*, 2, 1, 18–19.

Lindstromberg, S. (1990) *The Recipe Book*. Harlow, UK: Pilgrim Longman.

Lipa, L. (1990). Student and teacher perceptions of vocabulary difficulty. Paper presented at the National ELICOS Conference, Brisbane, Australia.

Long, M.H., & Porter, P.A. (1985). Group work, interlanguage talk and second language acquisition. *TESOL Quarterly*, 19, 2, 207–28.

Maingay, P. (1988). Observation for training, development or assessment? In Duff, T. (ed.), *Explorations in Teacher Training – Problems and Issues*. Harlow, UK: Longman.

Nunan, D. (1989). *Designing Tasks for the Communicative Classroom*. Cambridge: Cambridge University Press.

Prabhu, N.S. (1987a). Equipping and enabling. Paper presented at the RELC Conference, Singapore.

Prabhu, N.S. (1987b). *Second language pedagogy*. Oxford: Oxford University Press.

Richards, J.C. (1989). Beyond training: approaches to teacher education in language teaching. Keynote address given at workshop on second language teacher education, Macquarie University, Sydney, June 1989.

Richards, J.C. (1990). The dilemma of teacher education in second language teaching. In Richards, J.C. & Nunan, D. (eds.), *Second Language Teacher Education*. New York: Cambridge University Press.

Richards, J.C. & Nunan, D. (1990). *Second Language Teacher Education*. New York: Cambridge University Press.

Richards, J.C. & Rodgers, T.S. (1986). *Approaches and Methods in Language Teaching*. New York: Cambridge University Press.

Rogers, J. (1982). The world for sick proper. *English Language Teaching Journal*, 36, 3.

Rutherford, W.E. (1987). *Second Language Grammar: Learning and Teaching*. Harlow, UK: Longman.

Schön, D. (1983). *The Reflective Practitioner: How Professionals Think in Action*. Temple Smith.

Sinclair, J. & Coulthard, M. (1975). *Towards an Analysis of Discourse*. Oxford: Oxford University Press.

Smith, F. (1971). *Understanding Reading*. New York: Holt, Rinehart and Winston.

Stevick, E.W. (1980). *Teaching Languages: A Way and Ways*. Rowley, Mass: Newbury House.

Tollefson, J.W. (1989). A system for improving teachers' questions. *English Teaching Forum*, 27, 1, 6–9.

Tyler, C. (1989). Ghosts behind the blackboard: an exercise in teacher self-awareness. *The ELICOS ASSOCIATION News*, 7, 1.

Wajnryb, R. (1989). Stepping in gently: training the trainers. *EFL Gazette*, Nov. 1989.

(1991). The long arm of the Vaupes River Indian: applications of the silent phase to teacher training. *Prospect*, 6, 3, 50–7.

(1992). Risk taking for the timid teacher. *Cross Currents*, 18, 2, 153–6.

Weintraub, E. (1989). Look back and learn: the 'ghosts' behind the chalkboard. *TEA News*, 7, 1.

Widdowson, H.G. (1990). *Aspects of Language Teaching*. Oxford: Oxford University Press.

Williams, M. (1989). Processing in teacher training. Paper presented at IATEFL, Warwick.

Willing, K. (1988). *Learning Styles in Adult Migrant Education*. National Curriculum Resource Centre Adelaide, Australia.

Willis, J. (1981). *Teaching English through English*. Harlow, UK: Longman.

Woodward, T. (1989). Observation tasks for pre-service trainees. *The Teacher Trainer*, 3, 1, 25.

Woodward, T. (1991). *Models and Metaphors in Language Teacher Training*. Cambridge: Cambridge University Press.

Wright, T. (1987). *Roles of Teachers and Learners*. Oxford: Oxford University Press.

Zamel, V. (1981). Cybernetics: a model for feedback in the ESL classroom. *TESOL Quarterly*, 15, 2, 149.

# Task index

# Task index

# Index